N O P

D0131024

Q R S

T U V W

THE BEATLES

A to Z

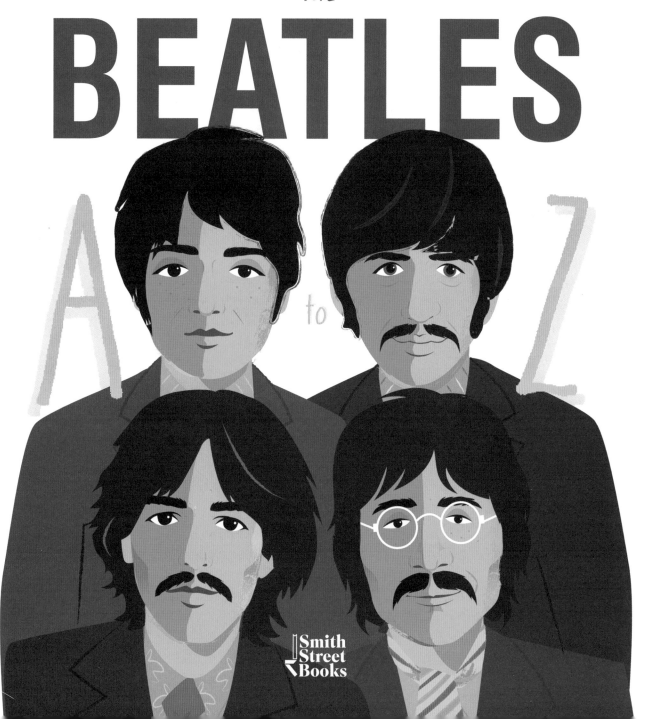

Smith
Street
Books

INTRODUCTION

The Beatles need little introduction. They are the highest-selling, most popular and most influential band in music history. They are Liverpool's greatest export and a linchpin of contemporary culture. Just hearing the name immediately conjures up images, names, phases and moments: the Fab Four, mop tops, coordinated stage bows, Indian meditation retreats, beads and kaftans, 'bigger than Jesus', Sgt. Pepper, the Abbey Road zebra crossing, 'Paul is dead' conspiracies, and so much more. The Beatles have provided pop culture with so many iconic moments. Most people have a favourite Beatles song and many also have a pivotal life event that is forever called up in their memory when they hear *that* song.

In the relatively short space of eight years, the Beatles changed the face of rock-and-roll and pop music forever. Restlessly inventive, precociously skilled, and with an uncanny an ear for melody, John, Paul, George and Ringo were to become almost a parody of a band. Theirs was a brand new kind of fame, and the foursome would continue to resonate even as pop music mutated and blurred across the fragile cultural divide of the 20th and 21st centuries.

At the heart of the dynamic was contemporary music's greatest songwriting partnership, Lennon–McCartney, a highly creative and eventually volatile collaboration, that produced many of modern music's best songs, but ended in a ball of flames.

The band had an enthusiastic and eager, almost naïve, beginning, which slowly succumbed to the onslaught of fame – the trappings of which became less and less important to the Beatles as they strove to retreat from constant media and fan attention.

The Beatles were at the forefront of revolutionary studio techniques (aided by producer George Martin and a slew of clever and inventive engineers), challenging the accepted norms of pop and rock. They revolutionised songwriting structures and were a band who wrote their own material – before the Beatles, songs were mostly written by experts for other people to sing. The band's constant desire not to stagnate or rest on their laurels led them to be at the forefront of music videos, and to invent the concept album, psychedelic rock and chiming indie melodic pop – they even predicted punk and metal. They changed the face of the cinema biopic, took animation to the level of art form and the pop band into a defiant gang who could vocalise their own frustrations with an uncaring world.

The Beatles A to Z performs a deep dive into the Beatles' history to uncover some lesser-known facts, anecdotes and fascinating details hiding under the many layers of famous and infamous Beatles stories, songs and albums – moments so embedded in contemporary culture that it's impossible now to imagine the progression of popular music without them.

STEVE WIDE

A

is also for

Australia

When the Beatles hit Australia in 1964, they kick-started the swinging sixties Down Under. Ringo missed part of the tour due to tonsillitis, so drummer Jimmie Nicol stood in for four days of fame. In Adelaide, 300,000 people turned out to greet them. It was the biggest crowd the Beatles ever had.

...

Abbey Road

This 11th studio album is an arresting mish-mash of styles. The last few tracks of the album are run together, culminating in the exquisite crescendo of 'The End'. Most of the recording had already been done for their last album, *Let It Be*, so the final day of mixing and editing *Abbey Road*, 20 August 1969, was the last time all four Beatles were in the studio together. The album also includes two of the best songs ever written, Harrison's 'Something' and 'Here Comes the Sun'.

...

Awards

During their career (and after) the Beatles racked up many awards. They won an Academy Award for Best Music (Original Song Score) for *Let It Be* in 1971. They won a total of four Brit Awards, including Oustanding Contribution to Music in 1977 and 1983. In 2014 they won a Grammy Lifetime Achievement Award and the Grammy Trustees Award in 1972, as well as seven other Grammys. They have also received a total of 19 Ivor Novello Awards and 17 NME Awards. They were entered into the Rock and Roll Hall of Fame in 1988, and the UK Music Hall of Fame in 2004.

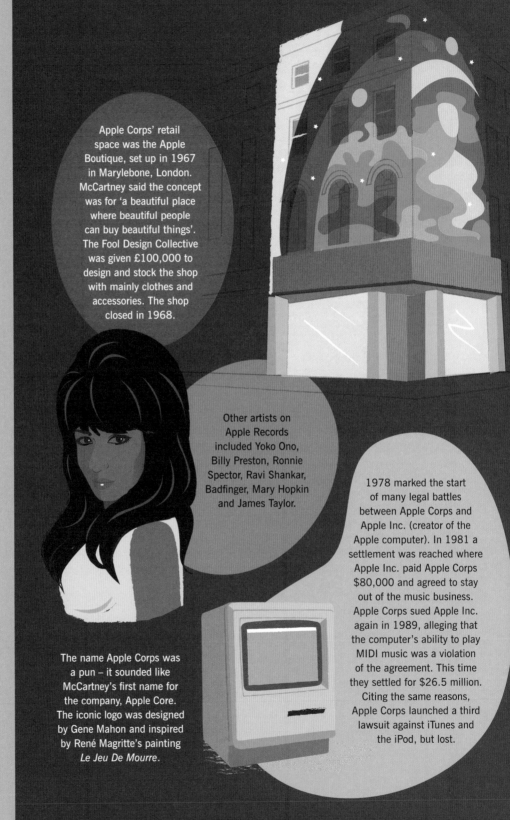

Apple Corps' retail space was the Apple Boutique, set up in 1967 in Marylebone, London. McCartney said the concept was for 'a beautiful place where beautiful people can buy beautiful things'. The Fool Design Collective was given £100,000 to design and stock the shop with mainly clothes and accessories. The shop closed in 1968.

Other artists on Apple Records included Yoko Ono, Billy Preston, Ronnie Spector, Ravi Shankar, Badfinger, Mary Hopkin and James Taylor.

1978 marked the start of many legal battles between Apple Corps and Apple Inc. (creator of the Apple computer). In 1981 a settlement was reached where Apple Inc. paid Apple Corps $80,000 and agreed to stay out of the music business. Apple Corps sued Apple Inc. again in 1989, alleging that the computer's ability to play MIDI music was a violation of the agreement. This time they settled for $26.5 million. Citing the same reasons, Apple Corps launched a third lawsuit against iTunes and the iPod, but lost.

The name Apple Corps was a pun – it sounded like McCartney's first name for the company, Apple Core. The iconic logo was designed by Gene Mahon and inspired by René Magritte's painting *Le Jeu De Mourre*.

A is for APPLE

Apple Corps Ltd, a company specialising in music publishing, films, electronics and retail, was founded by the Beatles in London in 1968. Lennon said, on forming the company, 'Our accountant came up and said, "We got this amount of money. Do you want to give it to the government or do something with it?"' After dissolving their existing company, The Beatles Ltd (the company under which they worked with Brian Epstein prior to his death in 1967), they formed The Beatles & Co., of which each member of the Beatles owned a five per cent share. Apple Corps would have control of the remaining 80 per cent. Lacking business acumen, the Beatles made a hash of their accounts and were often exploited by their employees, who would spend cash on drugs, booze and fine dining. The Fab Four would actually take it in turns to sit in the office pretending to be in charge while having no idea what they were doing. After several (failed) attempts to run the business themselves, the Beatles employed American business supremo Allen Klein as their manager and he set about streamlining the business. When the Beatles' partnership officially dissolved in 1975, the band retained control of Apple Corps. The current CEO is Jeff Jones and the business reportedly nets the surviving Beatles and the estates of John Lennon and George Harrison £67,000 per day, despite not owning the Beatles' back catalogue.

B is for BEATLEMANIA

The obsessive fan following for the Beatles, which came to be known as 'Beatlemania', is legendary within the annals of pop music. The term has been traced back to various sources in 1963, within months of the band's debut LP: in Vincent Mulchrone's article 'This Beatlemania' in the *Daily Mail* on 21 October; the 'BEATLEMANIA!' headline in the *Daily Mirror* on 2 November; Scottish music promoter Andi Lothian claims that he coined the phrase while speaking to a reporter on 5 October; and Tony Barrow, publicist to the Beatles, reportedly credited it to the press at the October London Palladium shows. It seems likely that the height of Beatlemania was during their tour of Europe, the United States, Hong Kong, Australia and New Zealand in 1964. What did the Beatles think of Beatlemania? George Harrison said, 'The more fame we got, the more girls came to see us, everybody making a noise so that nobody could hear us.' Beatlemania continued in varying degrees until the break-up in 1970, despite the band not touring from 1968 onwards.

Super-fan Jan Myers said in a *Japan Times* interview, 'We were fanatical. We could stand outside Abbey Road for 16 hours and as long as one of them came and smiled or said something it was fine.'

When the Beatles appeared on *The Ed Sullivan Show* in the US on 9 February 1964, 73 million viewers tuned in – 34 per cent of the population. Within the nine days of the Beatles US tour, it's estimated that Americans bought two million records.

It's hard to think of the Beatles without images of them hurtling down a main street with screaming fans running behind them, or performing on stage virtually inaudible amid the rapturous noise of the crowds.

The term 'mania' in reference to obsessive fandom had been used as early as the 1840s when composer Franz Liszt inspired a similar devotion to the Beatles. The Bay City Rollers would later garner the term 'Rollermania' in the early 1970s and the Spice Girls enjoyed a fleeting 'Spicemania' headline in the late nineties.

B is also for

Back catalogue
The history of the ownership of the Beatles' back catalogue is a complex story. However, the most famous owner was probably Michael Jackson, who bought the rights to the company ATV Music in 1985 – rights that included 250 Lennon–McCartney songs. After Jackson's death, ATV was purchased by Sony. In 2017 Paul McCartney filed a suit against Sony in an attempt to regain the rights to the Beatles' back catalogue.

...

'Back in the U.S.S.R.'
This opening track from *The Beatles (The White Album)* was McCartney's satirical response to the perfectly tanned vision of the Beach Boys' 'California Girls' and Chuck Berry's 'Back in the USA'. However, Berry was a major inspiration for the Beatles and, after Berry's death, McCartney stated, 'It's not really possible to sum up what he meant to all us young guys growing up in Liverpool.'

...

David Bailey
Uber-cool swinging sixties photographer David Bailey added the Beatles to his list of subjects for his famous *Box of Pin-Ups* portfolio of photographs, a series of crisp black-and-white portraits in 1965. Bailey told *GQ* magazine about the obvious tensions between Lennon and McCartney during the sessions, and how he'd eventually had to pose them back to back. Later he would have similar problems with Noel and Liam Gallagher of Oasis.

C
is also for

'Come Together'

Lennon's opening gambit on *Abbey Road* set the template for his future solo recordings. The jittery low-slung bass groove is instantly recognisable. The song was written for the Timothy Leary campaign to become governor of California, and the title was taken from his slogan. The campaign ended when Leary was jailed for marijuana possession. Disturbingly, Lennon can be heard in the intro whispering, 'Shoot me.'

...

Capitol Records

Beatles recordings were released through Capitol Records in the US, sparked off by the popularity of 'I Want to Hold Your Hand'. America famously had its own versions of Beatles records, some of which have become collectors' items.

...

Cover versions

The Beatles covered well over sixty songs. Early albums were peppered with covers, but even when they covered songs, the Beatles made them their own – cases in point: 'Twist and Shout', 'Dizzy Miss Lizzy', 'The Hippy Hippy Shake', 'Long Tall Sally' and 'Roll Over Beethoven'.

...

Eric Clapton

Clapton had a long association with the Beatles. When Harrison left the Beatles in 1969, Lennon wanted Clapton to replace him, saying, 'He's just as good and not such a headache.'

Although it wasn't a concert performance, their most famous live show was arguably the impromptu *Let It Be* concert on the rooftop of the Apple Corps offices in 1969 – to be imitated by U2 many years later in the video for 'Where the Streets Have No Name'.

Super-fan Maureen Lipman described cleaners from a concert in Hull finding 'forty pairs of abandoned knickers'!

In November 1963 the Beatles played the Royal Variety Performance and Lennon made his famous quip, 'The people in the cheaper seats, clap your hands. And the rest of you, if you'd just rattle your jewellery.' Some broadcasts cut to the Queen Mother, who appeared amused by the joke. Lennon had apparently considered saying 'fucking jewellery', but changed his mind at the last minute.

For the band's first gig at The Cavern Club, George Harrison was nearly denied entry because he looked so young. After the gig, the band was paid £5. Today the Beatles are said to bring in £82 million a year to the Liverpool economy.

The Beatles' final ticketed gig was at Candlestick Park, San Francisco, a 42,000-seat venue. However, only 25,000 tickets were sold – probably because the Beatles fell out of favour after Lennon's famous 'bigger than Jesus' comment. Tickets were $4.50 (general admission) or $6.50. The Beatles were paid $90,000.

The Hollywood Bowl was another watershed moment: the setting for the famous Beatles live album, *The Beatles at the Hollywood Bowl*, recorded over three nights in 1964 and '65.

is for

CONCERTS

At the height of their fame, Beatles concerts were riotous affairs where hordes of teens crammed massive stadiums and screamed their lungs out, missing pretty much every nuance of the Beatles' skillful guitar work and songwriting. But it took its toll and the Beatles would eventually stop touring altogether – but not before they had a few of pop music's pivotal performances under their belts. Famous Beatles concerts can be boiled down to some truly spectacular history-making events. There is the band's (possibly) first gig as the Beatles, with Pete Best on drums, on 5 January 1961 at the Litherland Town Hall in Merseyside. After that, The Casbah Coffee Club and the The Cavern Club became staple venues in Liverpool. Hamburg hosted them in venues such as the Kaiserkeller and Top Ten clubs. In 1963 they played the London Palladium as part of the popular show *Sunday Night at the London Palladium*. In January 1964 they played an extensive run at the Olympia Theatre in Paris, reportedly notching up a staggering 41 shows in 18 days. The Coliseum in Washington in February 1964 marked the Beatles' first live US performance (post-*The Ed Sullivan Show*) and was attended by 8000 fans. Their concert at New York's Shea Stadium in 1965 was attended by 50,000 people.

D is for DISCOGRAPHY

Please Please Me
March 1963

Beatles for Sale
December 1964

Help!
August 1965

Rubber Soul
December 1965

Revolver
August 1966

With the Beatles
November 1963

A Hard Day's Night
July 1964

The Beatles notched up many studio albums during their career, as well as countless bootlegs, live albums, compilations and EPs. They amassed 22 singles and 13 EPs. The actual album count is complex. In the UK the Beatles released 12 albums, but stereo and mono versions, reworks for international versions, and soundtracks that became albums change the landscape when the list is viewed in its entirety. For the purposes of this discography we'll go by the official UK albums, as the variants are all based on them. Of note is the 1962 album *My Bonnie*, by rock-and-roll musician Tony Sheridan, which is often considered the first Beatles record as it featured an outfit called 'The Beat Brothers' that comprised John Lennon, Paul McCartney, George Harrison, Stu Sutcliffe and Pete Best. Astoundingly, there is no gap year between any Beatles release. Up until *Revolver* in 1966 there

Abbey Road
September 1969

**The Beatles
(The White Album)**
November 1968

The BEATLES

**Sgt. Pepper's Lonely
Hearts Club Band**
June 1967

**Yellow
Submarine**
January 1969

Let It Be
May 1970

US-only releases
Meet the Beatles! (1964)
The Beatles' Second Album (1964)
Something New (1964)
The Beatles' Story (1964)
Beatles '65 (1964)
The Early Beatles (1965)
Beatles VI (1965)
Yesterday and Today (1966)
Magical Mystery Tour (1967)
Hey Jude (1970)

is also for

'Dear Prudence'
Mia Farrow and her sister Prudence accompanied the Beatles on their famous Indian meditation retreat in 1968. Prudence meditated for weeks in her room and wouldn't come out when called, inspiring the song 'Dear Prudence'. Prudence Farrow now teaches Transcendental Meditation in Florida.

...

'Drive My Car'
Used as the opener for *Rubber Soul*, 'Drive My Car' was mostly written by McCartney with some lyrics by Lennon. McCartney commented that 'drive my car' was blues slang for sex. It has also been suggested that the song refers to Epstein signing Cilla Black and her boyfriend Bobby Willis. Black reportedly objected to her boyfriend being signed up, instead saying that he could 'drive my car'.

...

Disney World
The Beatles officially ended at Disney World. On 29 December 1974 John Lennon signed the contract for the dissolution of the band, while staying at the Polynesian Village Hotel at Disney World.

...

Bob Dylan
The Beatles had always cited Dylan as a major influence and, in August 1964, they came face to face in the Delmonico Hotel in New York. The popular story describes the Beatles having joints for the first time. Dylan made a call to the lobby, yelling, 'This is Beatlemania!' True or not, the impact of the meeting was pivotal – the Beatles went on to write songs based on personal experience and Dylan started to use the electric guitar.

were two releases per year, a feat that was replicated in 1969 with *Yellow Submarine* and *Abbey Road*. This was a phenomenal output in a startlingly short space of time. From the beginning, the Beatles incorporated originals and covers. *Please Please Me* featured eight Lennon–McCartney songs and *With the Beatles* included seven, as well as the George Harrison–penned, 'Don't Bother Me'. However, the third album, *A Hard Day's Night*, was entirely made up of Lennon–McCartney compositions, while *Beatles for Sale* went back to the format of including eight originals mixed with covers – although the originals were by now starting to truly outshine the covers.

is also for

'The End'

The big finish to *Abbey Road* is a culmination of the intertwined tracks that make up the bulk of the B-side. The 'linked' tunes, a development of ideas explored on *Sgt. Pepper's*, was a revelation. The production was amazing and the famous, drawn-out orchestral sting at 'the end' of the track made history. Lennon said of the lyrics: 'Paul … He had a line in it, "And in the end, the love you take is equal to the love you make", a very cosmic, philosophical line … proves that if he wants to, he can think.'

…

Elvis

The Beatles were fans of Elvis, whom they met in 1965. Elvis continued to extol their virtues in public, despite the Beatles' press officer Tony Barrow recalling that Lennon opened the exchange with, 'Why do you do all these soft-centred ballads for the cinema these days? What happened to good old rock 'n' roll?'. Guitars came out and a jam session ensued. Gossip has always held that Elvis shot his TV screen when the Beatles came on. However, Graceland spokesman Kevin Kern says it was actually Robert Goulet.

…

'Eight Days a Week'

This track from *Beatles for Sale* went to number one in the US. It's also notable for being the first time in pop music that a song 'fades in' at the beginning. The title came from a chauffeur who was driving McCartney. McCartney asked the driver how he'd been and he replied, 'Working eight days a week.'

Epstein's various addictions included alcohol, pills and gambling. He would often lose large amounts of money and once reportedly placed a bet with a £100 cigarette lighter – which he lost. He was also known to take LSD and to smoke cannabis.

Epstein was instrumental in getting the Beatles their first recording contract. Despite the band being knocked back by many London record labels, George Martin, then the head of EMI Parlophone, signed them up – albeit reluctantly. He was impressed by Epstein's unwavering belief in the band and, it has to be said, by the fact that Epstein owned one of Liverpool's biggest record stores, NEMS, and might be hesitant to stock EMI products if refused.

Epstein first saw the Beatles on the cover of *Mersey Beat* and went to watch them play at The Cavern Club during a lunchtime performance in 1961. He later said, 'I was immediately struck by their music, their beat and their sense of humour on stage – and, even afterwards, when I met them, I was struck again by their personal charm.'

Brian Epstein invented the Beatles' synchronised bow at the end of their performances, imitated by a generation of bands.

In Lennon's famous 1970 *Rolling Stone* article, he said that when Epstein died he realised that it was the start of the Beatles' eventual demise. He said, 'I knew that we were in trouble then … I thought, "We've had it now".'

is for

BRIAN
EPSTEIN

Brian Epstein first saw the Beatles at The Cavern Club in Liverpool in November 1961, then went to see them perform at every gig for the next three weeks until finally offering to manage them on 3 December. In January 1962 the band (with Pete Best on drums) signed a five-year contract, which meant that Epstein earned 10–15 per cent of their income. In October they renegotiated, giving Epstein a cut depending on how much he earned for the band (after expenses). Epstein's management of the band saw several notable incidents, including the sacking of Pete Best, the signing of Lennon–McCartney to a publishing contract (Northern Songs), the signing of the Beatles' first recording contract, and organising the Beatles' final concert at Candlestick Park. Throughout his life and career, Epstein's homosexuality was kept secret despite being widely known within the Beatles' inner circle. At the age of 32 Epstein died of an overdose of the sleeping pill Carbitral combined with alcohol. His death was ruled an accident. While the band didn't attend the funeral for fear their fame would disrupt the occasion with a circus of media and fans, they did attend the memorial service held at the New London Synagogue. When the Beatles received their MBEs in 1965, Epstein was overlooked, not being part of the band. George Harrison remarked later that MBE stood for 'Mister Brian Epstein'. He was inducted into the 'non-performers' section of the Rock and Roll Hall of Fame in 2014.

is for

FIFTH BEATLES

The Beatles were four people – the 'Fab Four', in fact: a precociously talented, tight-knit unit that outsiders often found hard to break into, even socially. However, no fab four is an island and, along the way, they were complemented by many talented musicians, extraordinary agents, producers, business managers, engineers, associates and crew. Many were self-proclaimed 'fifth Beatles', some were dubbed by the press; and some were spiritually inducted by fans, commentators or music writers. It's worth noting that the Beatles themselves only ever called four people 'the fifth Beatle'. After George Martin's death, Paul McCartney wrote on his blog that 'If anyone earned the title of the fifth Beatle it was George'. Reportedly George Harrison named two people as being worthy of the title 'fifth Beatle': public relations manager Derek Taylor and Neil Aspinall, the Beatles' road manager (who would later become CEO of Apple Corps). Other people who at one time or another earned the prestigious moniker include actual former band members Pete Best and Stu Sutcliffe, as well as Tony Sheridan, Billy Preston and Eric Clapton.

Former drummer in the five-piece line-up, and actually part of the band when they signed their first contracts and record deals, Pete Best is often referred to as the fifth Beatle. Ringo replaced Best on drums in August 1962, when Best was fired by Brian Epstein (at the request of the rest of band, who felt that he didn't fit in).

Tony Sheridan used the Beatles as his back-up band in Hamburg and on his LP *My Bonnie*, making his album the Beatles' first true studio recording as a band and earning him the prestigious title of fifth Beatle.

Bass player with the Beatles in their days as a club act in Hamburg, Stuart Sutcliffe has often been referred to as the fifth Beatle, mostly due to the fact that he played bass guitar for the band when they were a five-piece, making him an actual member. Although Sutcliffe had left the band, it wasn't until he died in 1962 that the Beatles officially became a four-piece, with McCartney taking over on bass.

Eric Clapton has been referred to as the fifth Beatle for his session work on 'While My Guitar Gently Weeps', and for replacing Harrison when he briefly left the band in 1969.

F is also for

Fab Four
The Beatles' press officer from 1962–68, Tony Barrow, came up with the 'Fab Four' hookline in one of their first press releases. The band came to hate the name and the mop-top image, but later George Harrison would recall it fondly in a song he co-wrote with ELO's Jeff Lynne, 'When We Was Fab', which also featured Ringo Starr.

...

'The Fool on the Hill'
Released in 1967, and appearing on the *Magical Mystery Tour* EP and album, this Beatles classic was inspired by Maharishi Mahesh Yogi. McCartney said, 'I think I was writing about someone like Maharishi. His detractors called him a fool. Because of his giggle he wasn't taken too seriously …'

...

Fashion
The most famous and influential Beatles fashion moments include leather jackets, the mop-top hairstyle, the mod suit (complete with skinny tie), Beatles boots (Cuban-heeled), military brass-band uniforms, beards and long hair, round spectacles, and Indian-style tunics with beaded necklaces.

...

'Free as a Bird'
Twenty-five years after the break-up of the Beatles, Yoko Ono was asked if she had any unrecorded John Lennon songs. She uncovered home demos of 'Free as a Bird' and 'Real Love' (originally called 'Real Life'). The surviving Beatles all contributed to the tracks. 'Free as a Bird' went to number two on the UK chart in 1995 (kept off the number one spot by Pulp's 'Disco 2000'). It was the second-last Beatles recording to be released. It won a Grammy Award and meant that the Beatles had a UK top 40 hit four decades in a row.

G is also for

'Get Back'

'Get Back', by Paul McCartney, was released as a single in 1969 and ended up as the final track on *Let It Be*. It went to number one in the UK and US and was the first Beatles track to be released in 'true' stereo. McCartney wrote the song in response to the rise of right-wing British politician Enoch Powell and his anti-immigration policies. 'Get Back' is famous for its video, an impromptu live performance (they played it three times) on top of the Apple Corps building in 1969.

...

'Glass Onion'

Appearing on side one of *The Beatles (The White Album)*, 'Glass Onion' is a playful number that pokes fun at all the conspiracy theories that had emerged since *Sgt. Pepper's*, especially 'Paul is dead'. It references previous songs including 'Strawberry Fields Forever', 'I Am the Walrus' (the Walrus was Paul!), 'The Fool on the Hill', 'Lady Madonna' and 'Fixing a Hole'. Lennon said, 'I was having a laugh because there'd been so much gobbledygook about *Pepper* – play it backwards and you stand on your head and all that'.

...

Guitars

Dhani Harrison describes his father George's guitars as 'family heirlooms'. They include the Rickenbacker 360, a rosewood Fender Telecaster and a Gibson J-160E acoustic. Harrison and Lennon had matching Sonic Blue Stratocasters, inspired by Buddy Holly. Lennon used a Rickenbacker 325 Capri early on and later favoured the Epiphone Casino. You can't think of early McCartney without picturing that Höfner 500/1 violin bass. Adolf Rickenbacker himself gave Paul a 400/1S left-handed bass. *Rolling Stone* named Harrison 11th on their list of the 100 greatest guitarists. (Lennon was ranked 55th.)

Harrison formed HandMade Films in 1978 with Denis O'Brien. Credited with helping get the British film industry through a bad patch in the eighties, HandMade Films released several cinema classics, including *Monty Python's Life of Brian*, *The Long Good Friday*, *Time Bandits*, *Mona Lisa* and *Withnail and I*.

Harrison and his second wife, Olivia, were attacked by Michael Abram at their home in December 1999. Abram stabbed Harrison 40 times before being rendered unconscious by Olivia, who struck him repeatedly with a lamp and a poker. A paranoid schizophrenic, Abram believed Harrison was an alien and that the Beatles were 'witches from Hell'. Harrison repeatedly shouted 'Hare Krishna' during the attack. He survived, famously quipping afterwards, '[He] wasn't a burglar, and he certainly wasn't auditioning for the Traveling Wilburys.'

David Crosby introduced Harrison to the music of Ravi Shankar in 1965, leading to an obsession with the sitar. Harrison eventually met Shankar and became his devoted student for a time.

George's first wife, Pattie Boyd, was one of the top fashion models of the sixties, and later a photographer. Harrison wrote 'Something' for Boyd, a dedication anyone would hold dear. Boyd's youthful interest in Transcendental Meditation influenced the Beatles and led to their infamous trip to India. Harrison's close friend Eric Clapton was infatuated with Boyd (who inspired his lovelorn scorcher 'Layla'). After Harrison and Boyd split, Pattie eventually married Clapton.

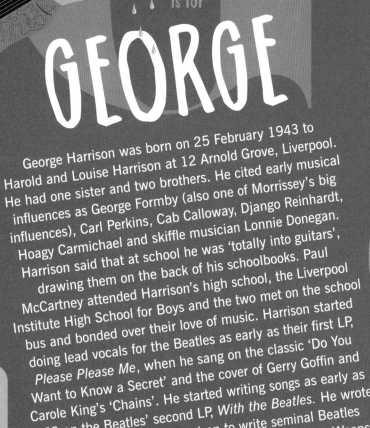

GEORGE

George Harrison was born on 25 February 1943 to Harold and Louise Harrison at 12 Arnold Grove, Liverpool. He had one sister and two brothers. He cited early musical influences as George Formby (also one of Morrissey's big influences), Carl Perkins, Cab Calloway, Django Reinhardt, Hoagy Carmichael and skiffle musician Lonnie Donegan. Harrison said that at school he was 'totally into guitars', drawing them on the back of his schoolbooks. Paul McCartney attended Harrison's high school, the Liverpool Institute High School for Boys and the two met on the school bus and bonded over their love of music. Harrison started doing lead vocals for the Beatles as early as their first LP, *Please Please Me*, when he sang on the classic 'Do You Want to Know a Secret' and the cover of Gerry Goffin and Carole King's 'Chains'. He started writing songs as early as 1963 on the Beatles' second LP, *With the Beatles*. He wrote 'Don't Bother Me' and went on to write seminal Beatles classics including 'Taxman', 'While My Guitar Gently Weeps', 'Here Comes the Sun' and 'Something', and the highly influential 'Within You Without You'. He spread his love of the guitar between the Fender, Rickenbacker and Gibson, as well as developing a keen interest in the sitar. Harrison became a Hindu and subsequently a vegetarian in the late sixties. Harrison died of lung cancer in 2001. His wife Olivia reported that his last words were 'Love one another'.

is for

HELTER
SKELTER

Track six on side three of the 1968 double LP *The Beatles (The White Album)*, 'Helter Skelter', has achieved historical notoriety for several reasons. McCartney had read an interview with Pete Townshend of the Who where Townshend described writing a song that was raw and dirty with a lot of echo ('I Can See for Miles'). Dogged by accusations of being a ballad or ditty writer, McCartney was inspired to go all out, writing a heavy guitar line, generating the most raw guitar sound he could and letting loose with one of his best vocal performances: a gritty, scratching, primal howl, shaping the future evolution of rock and roll, punk, hard rock and heavy metal. The Beatles remember the recording sessions as being lively and chaotic. Ringo (after the 18th take) can be heard at the end screaming, 'I've got blisters on my fingers.' A slower, more mellow version of the song was recorded, which lasted over 27 minutes, and a 12-minute version of the song was also recorded, later cut down to 4:37 for *Anthology 3*. The final version featured another influential touch – at 3:30 the song completely fades out, fades back in, out and in again before Ringo's famous outburst, a technique that has been emulated by many bands since. Ringo Starr later said, '"Helter Skelter" was a track we did in total madness and hysterics in the studio. Sometimes you just had to shake out the jams.' The track has no apocalyptic references or hidden messages, but American cult leader and murderer Charles Manson thought differently and used 'Helter Skelter' as the title for his 'apocalyptic war'.

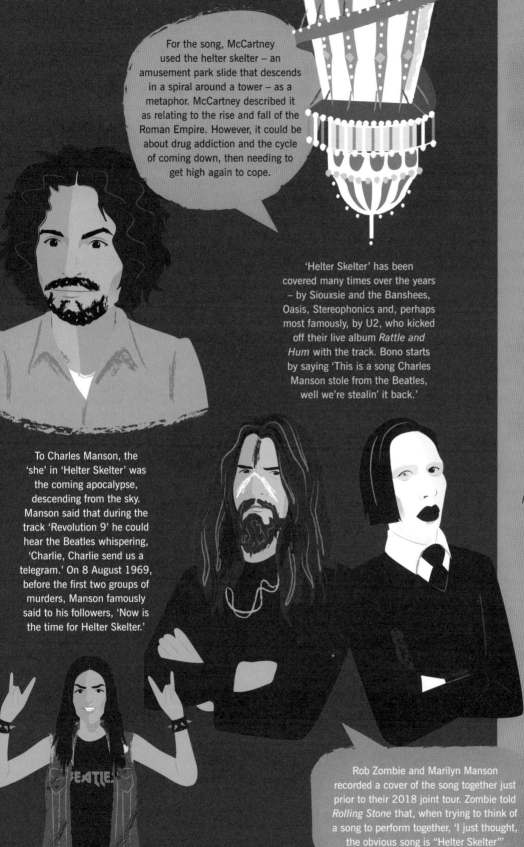

For the song, McCartney used the helter skelter – an amusement park slide that descends in a spiral around a tower – as a metaphor. McCartney described it as relating to the rise and fall of the Roman Empire. However, it could be about drug addiction and the cycle of coming down, then needing to get high again to cope.

'Helter Skelter' has been covered many times over the years – by Siouxsie and the Banshees, Oasis, Stereophonics and, perhaps most famously, by U2, who kicked off their live album *Rattle and Hum* with the track. Bono starts by saying 'This is a song Charles Manson stole from the Beatles, well we're stealin' it back.'

To Charles Manson, the 'she' in 'Helter Skelter' was the coming apocalypse, descending from the sky. Manson said that during the track 'Revolution 9' he could hear the Beatles whispering, 'Charlie, Charlie send us a telegram.' On 8 August 1969, before the first two groups of murders, Manson famously said to his followers, 'Now is the time for Helter Skelter.'

Rob Zombie and Marilyn Manson recorded a cover of the song together just prior to their 2018 joint tour. Zombie told *Rolling Stone* that, when trying to think of a song to perform together, 'I just thought, the obvious song is "Helter Skelter"'

H is also for

'A Hard Day's Night'
'A Hard Day's Night' is a classic Beatles single, their third LP and the name of their first film. The album and single went to number one in the UK, US, Germany and Australia. The title came from Ringo, who was known for his malapropisms (or 'Ringoisms'). The film was a smash hit and remains popular to this day.

...

Help!
Help! is the fifth studio LP from the Beatles, released in 1965. The title song is one of their enduring hits. Both the album and single went to number one in the UK, US and Australia. The album also featured 'You've Got to Hide Your Love Away', Ticket to Ride' and 'Yesterday'. It was also the title of the second Beatles film, *Help!*, released in the same year, which has had a lasting impact, especially as the template for many music videos.

...

'Here Comes the Sun'
One of George Harrison's two classics from *Abbey Road* (the other being 'Something'), 'Here Comes the Sun' has to be one of the Beatles' most optimistic songs. It kicks off side two, laying the template for the sun/harmony-drenched, conceptually linked B-side of the LP. Notably the song features an early use of the Moog synthesiser.

I
is also for

'I Am the Walrus'

One of the Beatles' greatest tracks was the B-side to 'Hello Goodbye', also included on the *Magical Mystery Tour* soundtrack. It held the number one and number two spots simultaneously, having been released as a single and in the double EP format – a unique feat in British singles chart history. The walrus in the song may have referred to Lewis Carroll's poem 'The Walrus and the Carpenter'. Various other obscure references and nonsense lyrics came from Lennon's imagination and events happening around him. 'Semolina pilchard' is said to refer to Sergeant Pilcher of the drug squad (the Beatles' arch-nemesis at the time). According to official biographer Hunter Davies, Lennon apparently said of the lyrics, 'Let the fuckers work that one out.'

...

'I Want to Hold Your Hand'

Written by Lennon–McCartney in 1963, this perennial Beatles tune would have been an easy number one (advanced orders alone were in excess of one million copies), but it was beaten to the top spot by 'She Loves You'. It eventually took over the number one slot, and stayed there for five weeks. 'I Want to Hold Your Hand' was the first Beatles tune to score a number-one hit in the US. Lennon mentioned that when they were writing the song, 'Paul hits this chord and I turn to him and say, "That's it! Do that again!"'

...

'Imagine'

Lennon's best-selling single, and arguably his most famous, was also the title of his 1971 post-Beatles album produced by Phil Spector. Before his death, Lennon said that Yoko Ono should receive a co-writing credit for the song. 'Imagine' is number three in *Rolling Stone*'s '500 Greatest Songs of All Time'.

George Harrison was the most keen of all the Beatles on Transcendental Meditation. Lennon remarked, 'The way George is going, he'll be flying a magic carpet by the time he's forty.'

While at the ashram, the Beatles were pitched a movie version of *Lord of the Rings*. Possible directors included Kubrick, Antonioni and David Lean. The director of the 2001 movie series, Peter Jackson, said that McCartney confirmed the story, saying that Paul was going to play Frodo; John would play Gollum; George was to play Gandalf and Ringo was slated for Sam.

The Beatles' Indian pilgrimage brought the practice of Transcendental Meditation to the world's attention and made the Maharishi very famous. However, a tearful Mia Farrow accused the Maharishi of inapropriate behaviour. The Beatles already had a feeling that their 'guru' was taking advantage of their fame and was trying to generate money, and the whole thing ended on a sour note, tarnishing the Maharishi's reputation forever. Harrison later stated that the group's suspicions of the Maharishi's behaviour were unfounded and he and Lennon apologised for the way they had treated him.

While in India, the singer Donovan taught John Lennon a method of finger-picking his guitar, which Lennon then passed on to Harrison. The style was used on the tracks 'Dear Prudence' and 'Julia'.

is for INDIA

In February 1968 the Beatles embarked on a pilgrimage to India. Inspired by a seminar on Transcendental Meditation given by the Maharishi Mahesh Yogi in the Welsh city of Bangor in 1967, the band travelled to Rishikesh in India's north to take part in a retreat at the Maharishi's ashram. Accompanied by their respective wives, girlfriends and assistants, as well as press, and sharing space with Mia Farrow, Donovan, and Mike Love from the Beach Boys, the Beatles (allegedly) gave up drugs and committed themselves to spirituality. The band displayed varying levels of interest and application to the TM sessions. Although Lennon was with his wife Cynthia on the trip, he became increasingly distant and sent daily postcards to Yoko Ono, whom he had started spending time with before the trip. The significance of those few months was huge. The band experienced one of their most creative periods of writing. It's estimated that more than 30 songs were written while they were there. They wrote nearly all of *The Beatles (The White Album)* and a couple of songs that appeared on *Abbey Road* and even on later solo albums. Most importantly, however, the short stay brought to light fractures within the group, which would lead to the band's break-up a year later. The ashram is now a tourist destination, referred to as 'The Beatles Ashram'.

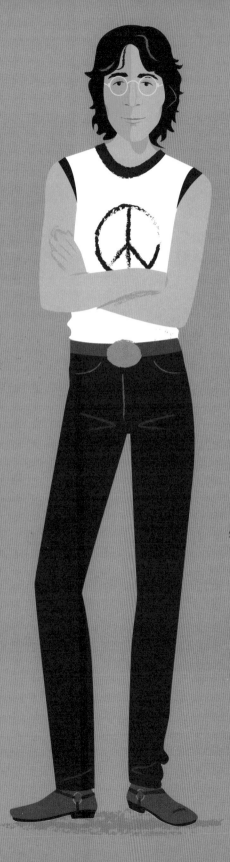

is for
JOHN

J

John Winston (Ono) Lennon was born on 9 October, 1940, in Liverpool to Alfred and Julia Lennon. With his father away at sea and his mother unable to cope, Lennon moved in with his mother's older sister Mimi and her husband George at 'Mendips', 251 Menlove Avenue. As his aunt and uncle had no children, Lennon had no live-in siblings, but was surrounded by aunts, uncles and cousins. He later said that although he didn't live with his mother, she visited regularly and, later, Lennon would say that he was brought up by 'five women that were my family. Five *strong, intelligent, beautiful* women, five sisters'. An avid fan of 'skiffle', Lennon formed his first band, the Quarrymen, in 1956, the nucleus of which would go on to become the Beatles four years later. A trouble-maker by his own admission, Lennon would continue to be controversial throughout his life. His caustic and insurgent personality saw him get in trouble repeatedly at school and later in public life, particularly for his views on the Vietnam War while he was living in the US. Along with Paul McCartney, he's regarded as being one half of the greatest songwriting partnership of all time. His career with the Beatles and subsequent solo works are among pop music's most popular releases. At the age of 40, Lennon was shot dead on 8 December 1980 in New York by Mark David Chapman.

WAR IS OVER

YES TO PEACE

Lennon's killer, Mark Chapman, shot Lennon five times. Lennon was his idol, but Lennon's offhand comment that the Beatles were 'bigger than Jesus', offended Chapman's religious sensibilities. Chapman remained at the crime scene reading *Catcher in the Rye* by JD Salinger (with which he was obsessed). He pleaded guilty to the charge of murder, despite his defence team's attempt to have him declared insane, and was sentenced to 20 years.

J.D SALINGER
THE CATCHER IN THE RYE

Lennon had two sons: Julian, with his first wife, Cynthia, and Sean, with his second wife, Yoko Ono. Both sons are musicians. Julian has been outspoken about his father's hypocrisy and neglect, saying, 'Dad could talk about peace and love out loud to the world but he could never show it to the people who supposedly meant the most to him: his wife and son'. Sean (born 1975) had a very different experience with his father – until Lennon's death in 1980 he was a full-time father to Sean.

An enduring legacy of John Lennon is his peace movement, a part-political, part-art statement made with his second wife, Yoko Ono. The 'Bed-Ins' were legendary events, where Ono and Lennon were photographed in bed, most famously in pyjamas holding flowers, but also making love, singing, conversing, creating and writing.

Julian Lennon
Julian was born in 1963 when Lennon was 23 and the band's career was really taking off. He inspired the songs, 'Lucy in the Sky with Diamonds', 'Hey Jude' and 'Goodnight'. In 1991 Julian had his own hit with the song 'Saltwater', about world peace and poverty, which reached number one in Australia and number six in the UK.

...

Jelly Babies
In 1962, Beatles fans took to throwing the English confectionery Jelly Babies at the band, as it had been reported that George Harrison liked them. Harrison implored fans to stop throwing the Jelly Babies after he was hit in the eye with one.

...

Jagger–Richards
Without a doubt, Lennon–McCartney and Jagger–Richards are two of the most powerful composing duos of all time. While Mick Jagger was the only real vocalist in the Stones, all Fab Four could sing. Apparently Richards told McCartney that the Stones were jealous of this. However, Jagger was not envious of the hysterical fans following the Beatles on their US tour. Jagger was one of the singers on 'All You Need Is Love', and he also inducted the Beatles into the Rock and Roll Hall of Fame in 1988.

K is also for

'Komm Gib Mir Deine Hand'/ 'Sie Liebt Dich'

In February 1964 the Beatles released a single in Germany – German versions of 'I Want to Hold Your Hand' and 'She Loves You'. 'Komm Gib Mir Deine Hand' actually translates to 'Give Me Your Hand'. 'Sie Liebt Dich' was also released in the US, where it went to number 97 on the charts.

...

Kids (biological)

John had two sons: Julian and Sean (both musicians); George had one son: Dhani (also a musician); Ringo has three kids: Zak and Jason, who have both pursued drumming, and Lee, who works in fashion; Paul has four children: Mary (a photographer and cookbook author), Stella (a very successful fashion designer), James (another musician), and Beatrice, the youngest of all the Beatles' offspring.

...

Knighthoods and honours

Despite all four members of the Beatles being awarded an MBE (in 1965), only two have knighthoods. Paul McCartney was knighted in 1997 and Ringo Starr in 2018. When the Beatles were awarded their MBEs, several other dignitaries returned their honours in disgust.

KAISERKELLER
FESTIVAL DER ROCK N ROLL FANS
OCTOBER – NOVEMBER – DEZEMBER
PRÄSENTIERT
BRUNO KOSCHMIDER
ORIGINAL
Rock n Roll
BANDS
Rory Storm
AND HIS
HVRICAN UND
The Beatles
ENGLAND – LIVERPOOL

Artist and photographer Astrid Kirchherr was introduced to the Beatles at the Kaiserkeller by her then-boyfriend Klaus Voorman. Kirchherr took the first professional photos of the Beatles, and became engaged to Stuart Sutcliffe.

At the Kaiserkeller the band were second-bill to another Liverpool band, Rory Storm and the Hurricanes, whose drummer was Ringo Starr. The bands played an outrageous five, sometimes six, 90-minute sets each night, reportedly relying on stimulants to get them through the marathon performances.

The co-founder of Hamburg's Star Club, Horst Fascher, went in search of a missing John Lennon one night just before he was due on stage. He found him in a bathroom 'engaged' with a woman and broke up the fun with a bucket of cold water. He told Lennon, 'I don't give a shit, you're going onstage and I don't care if you do it naked'. Lennon took the instruction literally and went on stage in his underpants with a toilet seat round his neck.

KAISER-KELLER

KAISERKELLER
FESTIVAL DER ROCK N ROLL TIME
OCTOBER · NOVEMBER · DECEMBER
PRÄSENTIERT
BRUNO KOSCHMIDER
ORIGINAL
Rock n Roll
BANDS
Rory Storm
AND HIS
HVRICAN
The Beatles
ENGLAND · LIVERPOOL

K is for

BRUNO KOSCHMIDER

In August 1960 a very young Beatles (including Stuart Sutcliffe on bass and Pete Best on drums), arrived in Germany to play 48 nights at the Indra club. The gig was organised by their then-manager Allan Williams, who booked UK bands to play residencies at entrepreneur Bruno Koschmider's clubs in Hamburg. The Indra was closed in early October due to noise complaints, so Koschmider moved the band to the more prestigious Kaiserkeller. The band bunked down in cramped, dirty rooms behind the screen at the sleazy Bambi Kino movie theatre (also owned by Koschmider). In *The Beatles Anthology* Harrison describes Koschmider: 'Bruno wasn't some young rock'n'roll entrepreneur, he was an old guy who had been crippled in the war. He had a limp and didn't seem to know much about music or anything. We only ever saw him once a week, when we'd try to get into his office for our wages.' It's estimated that the Fab Four spent around 1500 hours on stage in Hamburg and the band saw the time as an intense apprenticeship in rock and roll, with Lennon once famously stating, 'I might have been born in Liverpool, but I grew up in Hamburg.' The Beatles eventually moved to Peter Eckhorn's Top Ten club. Some think that it was Koschmider who informed the authorities that Harrison was only 17 and therefore ineligible to work, which led to Harrison's deportation. A few weeks later, Pete Best and Paul McCartney went to the Bambi Kino to collect their things and, while they were there, set fire to something. Koschmider felt the fire was intentionally started to burn down the cinema, and reported them, so they were imprisoned for attempted arson and later deported.

is for

LENNON-McCARTNEY

Pop music's best-known songwriting partnership, John Lennon and Paul McCartney, started composing songs almost as soon as they met in 1957. McCartney was impressed with John's band, the Quarrymen, and when asked to join he happily accepted. The two bonded over the Everly Brothers, Chuck Berry, Elvis, Buddy Holly, Little Richard and Smokey Robinson. They rehearsed the songs of their idols while taking the tentative steps towards writing their own material. They were highly collaborative, especially in the beginning, and differed from most songwriting partnerships in the fact that both wrote lyrics and music – whereas most duos (even Jagger–Richards) would have a lyricist and someone who wrote the music. They worked very closely together. Lennon described writing in the early days as 'eyeball-to-eyeball'. However, they would often write most of the songs separately before the other became involved. If one of them wrote a song, both would be credited, which is almost unheard of, and this arrangement continued until the Beatles split, and even in a couple of instances afterwards on solo records. Lennon later said that McCartney 'provided a lightness, an optimism, while I would always go for the sadness, the discords, the bluesy notes'. Between them they notched up an incredible 180-plus songs.

The bootleg album *A Toot and a Snore* featured a session between Lennon and McCartney in 1974 when McCartney dropped in while Lennon was producing Harry Nilsson's LP *Pussy Cats*. The name comes from a background comment by Lennon, 'You wanna snort, Steve? [Stevie Wonder] A? It's goin' round.' Lennon is on guitar and McCartney sings some harmony.

Liverpool

The British city of Liverpool is a major trade port. American rock and roll records would come in on the ships, giving the young Beatles a heads-up on the new sound. In 2016 it was estimated that the Beatles were still bringing in £82 million a year to the Liverpudlian economy. McCartney's and Lennon's family homes are now certified by the National Trust. McCartney stated in a *Playboy* interview in 1984: 'I never met anyone half as nice as some of the people I know from Liverpool … people who can just cut through problems like a hot knife through butter … Salt of the earth.'

…

Let It Be

The 12th and final Beatles album was released on 8 May 1970, a month after the band broke up. It went to number one in the UK and US and many other countries, and featured hits like the title track as well as 'Get Back' and 'The Long and Winding Road'. The bulk of it was written and recorded before *Abbey Road*, and was provisionally titled *Get Back*, but discontent within the band and the rejection of various mixes of the album led to it being shelved. When it was finally released, Phil Spector was brought in to remix some of the tracks. *Let It Be* garnered the Beatles their least favourable reviews.

…

Little Richard

Flamboyant singer Little Richard was a major influence on the early Beatles, in particular McCartney, who would imitate him at school. McCartney's early vocal style and head shake was a direct lift. Overall, the Beatles (and the Quarrymen) covered several Little Richard songs.

Ellie Greenwich, one of the songwriters from the famous Brill Building, the US hit factory of the 1960s said, 'When the Beatles and the entire British Invasion came in, we were all ready to say, "Look, it's been nice, there's no more room for us … It's now the self-contained group … What do we do?".'

Lennon–McCartney wrote songs for other bands and singers. Among them were the Rolling Stones' 'I Wanna Be Your Man' and Cilla Black's 'Love of the Loved' in 1963, Peter and Gordon's 'A World Without Love' in 1964, and Mary Hopkin's 'Goodbye' in 1969.

A classic example of Lennon and McCartney's distinct styles can be heard on 'A Day in the Life'. Lennon's melancholy verse structure is offset by Paul's jaunty middle refrain – the two parts coming together seamlessly.

M is also for

Magical Mystery Tour

A movie, a song, a double EP in the UK and an album in the US and Australia, *Magical Mystery Tour* is a whimsical flight of fancy, unscripted and loosely linked by six songs. The film was a critical failure, but the soundtrack went to number two on the UK charts. It was released as an LP in the US, with additional tracks put together from the Beatles' unreleased singles for 1967, and went to number one on the Billboard chart and was later nominated for a Grammy Award. The title track plus 'I Am the Walrus', 'Strawberry Fields Forever', 'Penny Lane', 'Hello Goodbye' and 'All You Need Is Love', all on the same album, make it one of the best collections of songs in the band's career.

...

'Michelle'

'Michelle' was written by McCartney and included on *Rubber Soul*. It was formed from an earlier song McCartney had written to mock some French students then reworked, with an added 'I Love You' bridge suggested by Lennon.

...

Mop top

The famous Beatles shaggy haircut – inspired by European bohemians of the time – got its name because of its resemblance to a mop. The style was also known among fans as 'Arthur', after a reporter asked George what he called his haircut.

Martin produced two of the enduring James Bond themes: Shirley Bassey's iconic 'Goldfinger' in 1964 and 'Live and Let Die' by Paul McCartney and Wings in 1973.

George Martin's oboe teacher was Margaret Eliot. Her stepdaughter Jane Asher would later become Paul McCartney's partner from 1963 to '68.

During their conversations, not being a fan of their original compositions or Pete Best's drumming, Martin asked the guys if there was anything that they themselves didn't like. Harrison quipped, 'Well, there's your tie for a start,' and the other Beatles joined in with a comic exchange.

The Beatles requested that Martin produce their single 'Please Please Me', which he did. However, he told them to speed it up – at the time it was a ballad. After the recording Martin said, 'Gentlemen, you have just made your first number one record.' (It did reach number one on some charts.)

Martin favoured the Telefunken Elektroakustik U48 Microphone and the Coles 4038 Studio Ribbon Microphone, Chandler RS124 Compressor and the REDD.47 Preamp.

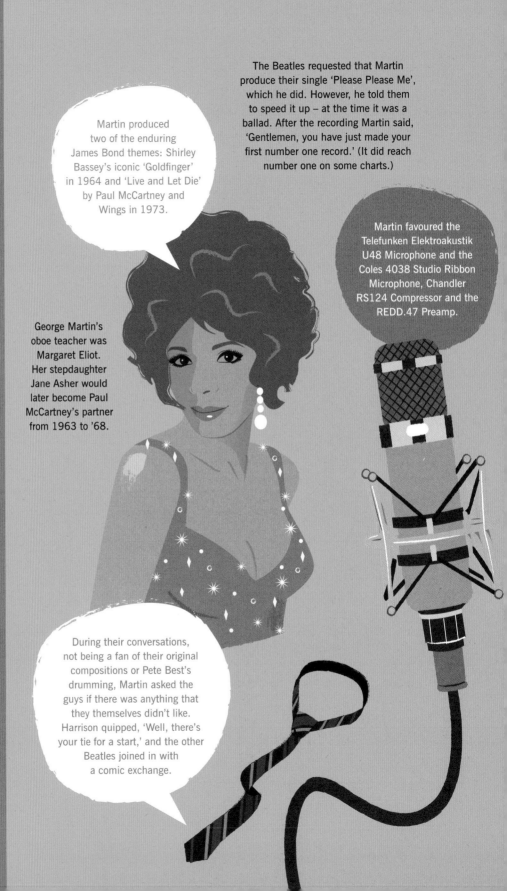

is for

GEORGE MARTIN

George Henry Martin was born on 3 January 1926 in Highbury, London. He studied piano and oboe at the Guildhall School of Music and harboured ambitions of becoming a composer. He worked for the BBC's classical music department before joining EMI records, becoming head of their subsidiary label Parlophone. He produced comedy records for Spike Milligan, Peter Sellers and the Goons, as well as classical releases and regional music. The Beatles had been turned down by Decca, but Brian Epstein spruiked them to a sceptical Martin. He responded to Epstein's enthusiasm after listening to a tape of the band and agreed to a meeting – he liked Lennon and McCartney's vocals, even though he thought the band held little promise. After negotiations, the band signed a contract with Martin and he was involved in the production of their UK albums from that point onward. Martin's innovation in sound-studio techniques included reversing and changing pitch on tape loops, panning and stereo manipulation, atmospheric recreation and emulation, spiky and raw guitar (early punk sounds), experimental soundscapes and cut-ups, and 'bouncing down', where more tracks were made available on limited machines by recording previous takes onto one track. Martin composed and arranged the score on the B-side of *Yellow Submarine*. His arrangements augmented tracks like 'Eleanor Rigby' and the highly influential orchestra meltdown at the end of 'A Day in the Life'. He also played with string and brass arrangements on 'I Am the Walrus' and 'Strawberry Fields Forever'. His ideas, however big or small, and his skills as a producer and engineer helped to shape the Beatles' sound.

N is for NUMBER ONES

Throughout their career, the Beatles amassed a total of 17 number-one singles in the UK, and 27 number-one singles if you factor in the US charts as well. In some instances the releases were double A-sides, which qualified both tracks to be counted as number one, for instance 'Day Tripper'/'We Can Work it Out'. The Beatles' first number one was – depending on which source you use – 'Please Please Me' in January 1963. However, it only reached number two on the Record Retailer Chart (later the official UK Singles Chart), viewed as the standard. As a result, 'From Me to You' is officially the Beatles' first number-one UK single, reaching the peak position on 24 April 1963. The Beatles' number-one singles (UK) were therefore: 'From Me to You' (April 1963), 'She Loves You' (September 1963), 'I Want to Hold Your Hand' (December 1963), 'Can't Buy Me Love' (January 1964), 'A Hard Day's Night' (July 1964), 'I Feel Fine' (September 1964), 'Ticket to Ride' (April 1965), 'Help!' (August 1965), 'Day Tripper'/'We Can Work it Out' (December 1965), 'Paperback Writer' (June 1966), 'Yellow Submarine'/'Eleanor Rigby' (August 1966), 'All You Need Is Love' (July 1967), 'Hello Goodbye' (December 1967), 'Lady Madonna' (March 1968), 'Hey Jude' (September 1968), 'Get Back' (April 1969) and 'The Ballad of John and Yoko' (June 1969). The total number of weeks that the Beatles' songs spent at number one on the UK charts during their career was 69. In 2000 the album *1 (One)* was released, compiling the Beatles' 27 number-one UK and US singles. True to its name, the compilation reached the number-one chart position in more than 20 countries.

'Hello Goodbye' was written by McCartney (a Gemini) about opposites within the universe, although it reportedly came about in a songwriting session with aide Alistair Taylor, where McCartney called out words and Taylor responded with the opposite.

Hello, hello, hello

Goodbye

'Hey Jude', released in 1968, was written by Paul to console the five-year-old Julian Lennon (the original title was 'Hey Jules') but also addressed the emerging John/Yoko and Paul/Linda relationships. George Martin thought the radio wouldn't play a seven-minute single, but Lennon said, 'They will if it's us.' It was their longest single to stay at number one in the US, at nine weeks. The catchy 'Na na na na' outro lasts for four minutes, longer than the main part of the song.

'The Ballad of John and Yoko' was the Beatles' last UK number-one single. Written by Lennon it reached the top of the charts in May 1969. Starr and Harrison weren't involved in the recording, but McCartney played drums. The song was banned by many US radio stations for featuring the words 'Christ' and 'crucify' in the chorus.

N is also for

Noises
The Beatles were known for their inventive techniques and this often involved the use of extraneous noise – background, percussive, ambient or atmospherics. Some of the Beatles' best noises include the reverse orchestral sting for the finale of 'The End', a secret high-pitched sound on *Sgt. Pepper's* that only dogs (and people with exceptional ears) can hear, the backwards tape-loop in 'Revolution 9' and at the end of 'I Am the Walrus', the feedback and amp buzz in 'I Feel Fine', and the carnival sounds on 'For the Benefit of Mr Kite'.

...

'Norwegian Wood'
From *Rubber Soul*, 'Norwegian Wood' was possibly shaped by the Beatles' meeting with Bob Dylan, who inspired them to write more about personal experiences. The lead sitar line inspired chart psychedelia and the sound of artists like Donovan. The song is said to be about Lennon's affair with Maureen Cleave or Sonny Freeman. McCartney explained that the 'wood' reference was a dig at cheap 1960s pine wall panelling, which was fashionable at the time.

...

NASA
On 4 February 2008 NASA beamed the song 'Across the Universe' into deep space towards the star Polaris, 431 light years from Earth. Paul McCartney sent a message to the space agency – 'Send my love to the aliens. All the best, Paul'.

O is also for

Other names

Before the Beatles were the Beatles, some of their names were the Blackjacks, the Quarrymen, Johnny and the Moondogs, the Beat Brothers, the Silver Beetles and the Beatals.

…

'Ob-La–Di, Ob-La-Da'

From *The Beatles (The White Album)*, this jaunty track probably ranks regularly as both the most loved and the most loathed Beatles song. Written by McCartney and inspired by reggae legend Desmond Dekker, the song has often been described as one of the worst songs of all time. However, it was a number-one single in several countries and has been covered by more than 30 artists, including Scottish popsters Marmalade, who took it to number one in the UK in 1968.

…

1 (One)

This Beatles' compilation of number-one singles was released in November 2000. It featured all their number-one hits and sold 31 million copies, making it the fourth highest–selling record that year, and the best-selling album in the US for the years 2000–2009.

The portrait of Ono and and a naked Lennon that appeared on *Rolling Stone*'s 22 January 1981 issue was taken by Annie Leibovitz on 8 December 1980 – just hours before Lennon was killed. The iconic image is one of the most famous photographs in the world. In 2005 the American Society of Magazine Editors voted the cover the best magazine cover of the previous 40 years.

John Lennon was shot and killed after he and Ono returned from a mixing session for Ono's 'Walking on Thin Ice', which she released three weeks later, dedicating it to John.

After Lennon's death, Ono never remarried. She worked to keep John's legacy alive, funding the Strawberry Fields memorial in Central Park, New York, and the Imagine Peace Tower in Iceland.

Following Lennon's death, Ono requested that John's memory be honoured with a 10-minute silent vigil. Tens of thousands gathered to participate in New York, Liverpool and other cities around the world, and some radio stations marked the occasion by temporarily halting their broadcasts.

HAIR PEACE

BED PEACE

Ono and Lennon famously spent their honeymoon protesting America's involvement in the Vietnam War, promoting peace and setting up Bed-Ins for Peace in Amsterdam and Montreal.

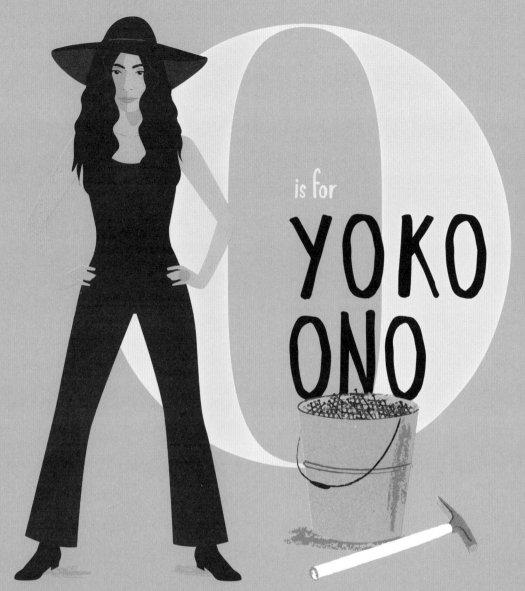

is for

YOKO ONO

Artist Yoko Ono was born on 18 February 1933. Although she grew up in Tokyo, she moved to upstate New York when she was 18. Her time in New York City from about the age of 20 helped to shape her approach to art and music. She was drawn to the arts scene in downtown New York, in particular the experimental group Fluxus. The official story of how Lennon and Ono met involved a sceptical Lennon visiting Ono's exhibition at the Indica Gallery in Mayfair, London, in 1966. One work, *Painting to Hammer a Nail In*, required the viewer to hammer a nail into a board. Lennon went to hammer the first nail in but, as the exhibition hadn't opened yet, he was stopped by Ono. Gallery owner John Dunbar said to Ono, 'Don't you know who this is? He's a millionaire! He might buy it.' Ono, who claimed to have never heard of the Beatles, said he could hammer the nail in if he gave her five shillings. Lennon replied, 'I'll give you an imaginary five shillings and hammer an imaginary nail in.' They officially became a couple in 1968 and married a year later. After a period of separation from 1973 to '75, Lennon and Ono got back together and later achieved commercial success with the release of the album *Double Fantasy* in 1980. Lennon was murdered just three weeks later. Although Ono has been repeatedly blamed by the press and some music historians for breaking up the Beatles, the band members have denied this. In an interview with Dick Cavett, Harrison said that there were problems within the Beatles camp long before Ono came along.

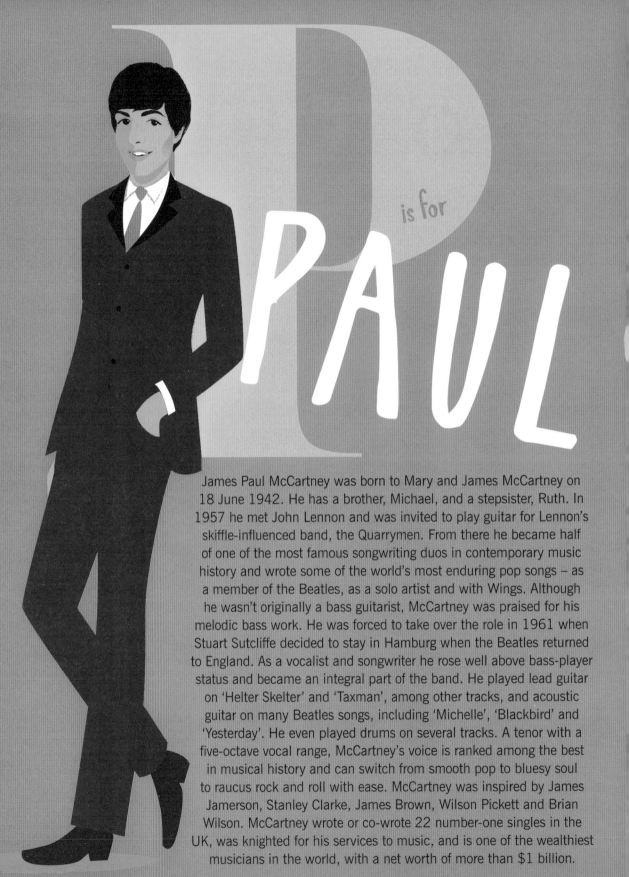

P is for PAUL

James Paul McCartney was born to Mary and James McCartney on 18 June 1942. He has a brother, Michael, and a stepsister, Ruth. In 1957 he met John Lennon and was invited to play guitar for Lennon's skiffle-influenced band, the Quarrymen. From there he became half of one of the most famous songwriting duos in contemporary music history and wrote some of the world's most enduring pop songs – as a member of the Beatles, as a solo artist and with Wings. Although he wasn't originally a bass guitarist, McCartney was praised for his melodic bass work. He was forced to take over the role in 1961 when Stuart Sutcliffe decided to stay in Hamburg when the Beatles returned to England. As a vocalist and songwriter he rose well above bass-player status and became an integral part of the band. He played lead guitar on 'Helter Skelter' and 'Taxman', among other tracks, and acoustic guitar on many Beatles songs, including 'Michelle', 'Blackbird' and 'Yesterday'. He even played drums on several tracks. A tenor with a five-octave vocal range, McCartney's voice is ranked among the best in musical history and can switch from smooth pop to bluesy soul to raucus rock and roll with ease. McCartney was inspired by James Jamerson, Stanley Clarke, James Brown, Wilson Pickett and Brian Wilson. McCartney wrote or co-wrote 22 number-one singles in the UK, was knighted for his services to music, and is one of the wealthiest musicians in the world, with a net worth of more than $1 billion.

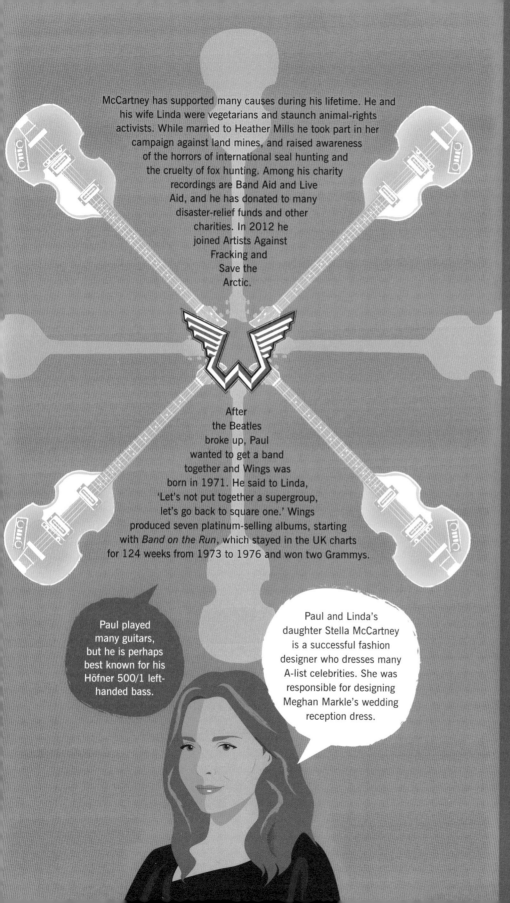

McCartney has supported many causes during his lifetime. He and his wife Linda were vegetarians and staunch animal-rights activists. While married to Heather Mills he took part in her campaign against land mines, and raised awareness of the horrors of international seal hunting and the cruelty of fox hunting. Among his charity recordings are Band Aid and Live Aid, and he has donated to many disaster-relief funds and other charities. In 2012 he joined Artists Against Fracking and Save the Arctic.

After the Beatles broke up, Paul wanted to get a band together and Wings was born in 1971. He said to Linda, 'Let's not put together a supergroup, let's go back to square one.' Wings produced seven platinum-selling albums, starting with *Band on the Run*, which stayed in the UK charts for 124 weeks from 1973 to 1976 and won two Grammys.

Paul played many guitars, but he is perhaps best known for his Höfner 500/1 left-handed bass.

Paul and Linda's daughter Stella McCartney is a successful fashion designer who dresses many A-list celebrities. She was responsible for designing Meghan Markle's wedding reception dress.

P is also for

Partners

Paul McCartney was in a six-year relationship with actress Jane Asher from 1963 to 1968. In 1969 he married Linda Eastman and they remained married until her death from breast cancer in 1998. He later married anti-landmine campaigner Heather Mills in 2002, but separated from her in 2006 and divorced in 2008. He has been married to New York freight company heiress Nancy Shevell since 2011. John Lennon was married to Cynthia Lennon (nee Cox) from 1962 to 1968, then married Yoko Ono in 1969. He separated from Ono in 1973 and had an affair with personal assistant May Pang before reuniting with Ono in 1975. George Harrison was married to Pattie Boyd from 1966 until 1977. A year later he married Olivia Arias. Ringo Starr was married to Maureen Cox from 1965 to 1975. He later married actress Barbara Bach, whom he met on the set of the movie *Caveman*. They have been married since 1981.

...

'Penny Lane'

Released as a double A-side with 'Strawberry Fields Forever', 'Penny Lane' was written by Paul McCartney and included on the US version of *Magical Mystery Tour*. Similar to Lennon's revisiting of his childhood in 'Strawberry Fields Forever', Paul sings about a street from his childhood in Liverpool and the characters he remembered. Paul said the song 'was kind of nostalgic, but it was really a place that John and I knew; it was actually a bus terminus. I'd get a bus to his house and I'd have to change at Penny Lane.'

Q is also for

Quincy

Famed record producer Quincy Jones took potshots at the Beatles in a 2018 *New York* magazine interview. He said, 'They were the worst musicians in the world … They were no-playing motherfuckers. Paul was the worst bass player I ever heard.' He then added, 'And Ringo? Don't even talk about it.' He then went on to talk about it, citing the time that he arranged 'Love Is a Many Splendoured Thing' for Ringo's 1970 album *Sentimental Journey*. Jones said, 'Ringo had taken three hours for a four-bar thing he was trying to fix on a song. He couldn't get it.' They sent him out to relax and got jazz drummer Ronnie Verrell to record the drums. When Ringo returned he listened to the take and said, 'That didn't sound so bad.' Jones replied, 'Yeah, motherfucker because it ain't you.'

…

Queen Elizabeth II

The Beatles had several encounters with Queen Elizabeth II, playing Royal Variety Performances and at a few other meetings, notably when the Queen awarded them each an MBE. Lennon later returned his medal but couldn't revoke his MBE status. Legend has it that at the time of their hippy transformation in 1967, the Queen said to the chairman of EMI, Joseph Lockwood, that the Beatles were 'turning funny'.

The Quarrymen played 'Worried Man Blues' at an audition for *TV Star Search* held at Liverpool's Empire Theatre. They were well received, but the Liverpudlian Sunnyside Skiffle Group's stagecraft outshone the inexperienced Quarrymen. After the competition, a clapometer was used to judge which band was more popular and, after a few attempts, the Quarrymen were beaten, but not by much.

The band's name has been attributed to both John Lennon and Pete Shotton, who attended Quarry Bank High School in Liverpool. The name was taken from a line in the school anthem: 'Quarrymen, old before our birth'.

The skiffle sound, which originated in the US, was a mix of jazz, folk and blues and was played on makeshift instruments, such as the washboard and tea chest bass, which could easily be put together even if you had little money.

Lennon and McCartney started writing songs while in the Quarrymen, albeit separately. Lennon wrote 'Hello Little Girl' and McCartney penned 'I Lost My Little Girl'. Both men were struck by the quality of each other's songs.

The Quarrymen formed in Liverpool in 1956. Briefly known as the Blackjacks, the band were exponents of the US-based 'skiffle' sound, which had become popular in Liverpool. The original Quarrymen were John Lennon, Eric Griffiths, Pete Shotton and Bill Smith, with incarnations including Nigel Walley, Ivan Vaughan, Len Garry, Colin Hanton and Rod Davis. Paul McCartney joined in October 1957 and George Harrison in 1958. In 1958 Griffiths left to join the navy, and Shotton left after Lennon broke a washboard over his head! As a trio, Lennon, McCartney and Harrison played under a few different names including Johnny and the Moondogs and Japage 3, before returning to the Quarrymen and making a recording with Hanton and Garry featuring Buddy Holly's 'That'll Be the Day' and a McCartney–Harrison composition, 'In Spite of All the Danger'. Lennon sang all the vocals. Some scratchy live recordings of early performances also exist. Garry was unable to play with the band again due to a long stay in hospital, and Hanton left after a fight. In 1960 the trio was joined by guitarist Ken Brown, but the band lacked bass or drums. Brown fell ill so Stuart Sutcliffe joined on bass. Pete Best was added on drums and, after it was agreed that the Quarrymen wasn't a name anyone really liked, the group eventually decided on the Beatles. The rest, as they say …

is for

THE QUARRYMEN

B is for **RINGO**

Richard Starkey was born on 7 July 1940 to Richard 'Dick' Starkey and Elsie Gleave and was an only child. His father left when he was young and his mother remarried Harry Graves. Ringo's relationship with Graves was good and his first 'drum kit' was a Christmas present from his stepfather. It was made up of a snare, a bass drum and a rubbish bin lid that acted as a cymbal. When the skiffle craze came along, Ringo became obsessed, and started to join bands. His tenure with popular Liverpool group Rory Storm and the Hurricanes saw him catch the attention of the Beatles and, in 1962, when Pete Best was fired as drummer, Ringo emerged as the top candidate to replace him – he had already played with the three Beatles in Hamburg and recorded with them. During Ringo's time with the Beatles he collaborated on songs, but only wrote two that were released by the band: 'Octopus's Garden' and 'Don't Pass Me By'. He sang vocals at least once on every album, and enjoyed a number-one hit that featured his vocals in 'Yellow Submarine'; and he also performed vocals on the classic 'With a Little Help from My Friends'. His contribution to the Beatles movies was considerable and he was admired by critics and audiences for his dry wit and sharp one-liners. Ringo became a keen photographer and was credited as director of photography for the *Magical Mystery Tour* movie.

Ringo was frequently hospitalised as a child, suffering from appendicitis and later, tuberculosis, causing him to miss a lot of school. When he returned to school after a prolonged absence, his classmates called him 'Lazarus'.

As one of the few drummers with an actual kit, Ringo became a member of Rory Storm and the Hurricanes in 1959, where he first adopted the name Ringo Starr. His break-out drum solos during the shows were known as 'Starr Time', something the Beatles continued to use in their set. His first proper drum kit in 1963 was a Ludwig Oyster Black Pearl three piece, which sold at auction in 2015 for US$2.25 million.

Sung by Ringo Starr (and written by him with help from George Harrison) 'Octopus's Garden' appeared on *Abbey Road*. It was inspired by Starr's time spent on Peter Sellers' boat in Sardinia, and the captain's stories about how octopods build their own gardens on the ocean floor. Starr later admitted that the song was also a plea to escape the problems within the Beatles, saying he 'just wanted to be under the sea, too'.

Though not popular at first, as Beatles fans were upset by Best's departure, Ringo eventually started receiving as much fan mail as the other group members. The lapel pins saying 'I Love Ringo' were 1964's hottest-selling Beatles item.

I LOVE RINGO

Ringo's son Zak Starkey is also a well-known drummer who has played with Johnny Marr, the Who, Oasis, Icicle Works, the Lightning Seeds and Paul Weller.

R is also for

'Revolution 9'
This infamous sound collage on *The Beatles (The White Album)* was created by Lennon with Yoko Ono and George Harrison. Lennon said his main idea was to 'paint' a revolution using sound. The experimental ending of the album version of 'Revolution' was the jumping-off point for this aural sculpture, inspired by Ono's art as well as works by avant-garde composers. Overdubs, tape loops, sound effects, spoken word and studio manipulation all created a thrilling and inventive work.

...

Rubber Soul
The sixth Beatles studio LP, from 1965, was the last released before their final concerts. It redefined the album as more than just a support for singles, being a collection of sophisticated, quality pop songs in their own right. It also started to introduce elements of psychedelia and prog rock. Key tracks include 'Drive My Car', 'Michelle', 'Norwegian Wood' and 'In My Life'.

...

Revolver
The Beatles' seventh UK studio LP, and the first since they stopped performing live, *Revolver* is the precursor to *Sgt. Pepper's*. Freed up from touring, the Beatles could spend more time in the studio and the results were electric – from the orchestration of 'Eleanor Rigby' and the psychedelic groove of 'Tomorrow Never Knows', to the expanded music palette on 'I'm Only Sleeping' and 'She Said, She Said'.

...

The Rutles
This parody of the Beatles was created by Monty Python's Eric Idle and comedian Neil Innes in two mockumentaries, *All You Need Is Cash* and *The Rutles 2: Can't Buy Me Lunch*.

S is also for

Stuart Sutcliffe

The original bass guitarist with the Beatles, Sutcliffe played with them during their time in Hamburg, Germany. He became enamoured with German photographer Astrid Kirchherr and the existentialist bohemian fashion stylings of her art school group, which in turn influenced the Beatles' look and sound. Along with Lennon, Sutcliffe is credited with coming up with the name 'the Beetles' (they were both big fans of Buddy Holly and the Crickets). Sutcliffe chose to remain in Germany with Kirchherr and sadly died of a brain haemorrhage in April 1962. If Sutcliffe had survived, his talent for painting may have seen him become famous in his own right. Sutcliffe appeared as one of the characters on the cover of *Sgt. Pepper's*. Yoko later said that John spoke of him often and once described Sutcliffe as his 'alter ego ... a spirit in his world ... a guiding force'.

...

'Something'

Harrison's love song for his then-wife Pattie Boyd was track two on 1969's *Abbey Road*. It won the Ivor Novello Award for best song in 1971.

...

'Sexy Sadie'

'Sexy Sadie', from *The Beatles (The White Album)*, was Lennon's takedown of the meditation guru the band had publicly spent time with in India. Disillusioned with what he thought was going to be a deeply spiritual awakening, Lennon wrote the line, 'Maharishi, what have you done' on hearing complaints of sexual impropriety from fellow meditator Mia Farrow. Harrison convinced Lennon to change the lyrics.

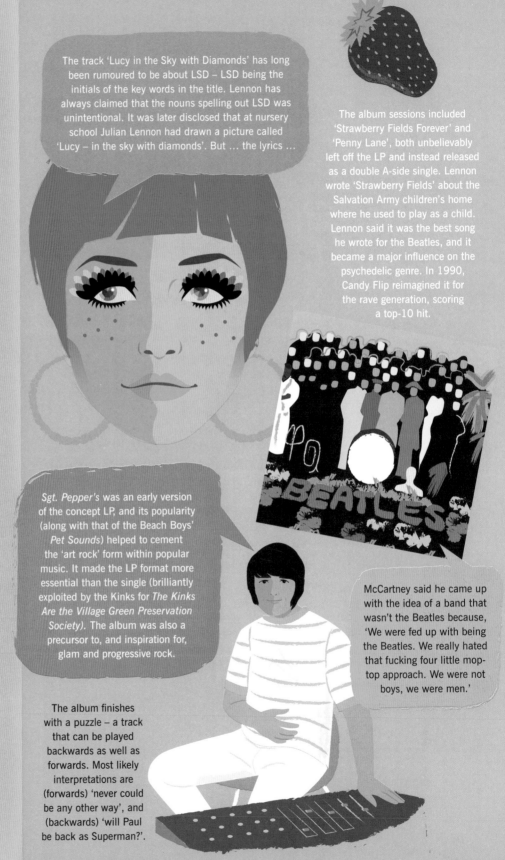

The track 'Lucy in the Sky with Diamonds' has long been rumoured to be about LSD – LSD being the initials of the key words in the title. Lennon has always claimed that the nouns spelling out LSD was unintentional. It was later disclosed that at nursery school Julian Lennon had drawn a picture called 'Lucy – in the sky with diamonds'. But ... the lyrics ...

The album sessions included 'Strawberry Fields Forever' and 'Penny Lane', both unbelievably left off the LP and instead released as a double A-side single. Lennon wrote 'Strawberry Fields' about the Salvation Army children's home where he used to play as a child. Lennon said it was the best song he wrote for the Beatles, and it became a major influence on the psychedelic genre. In 1990, Candy Flip reimagined it for the rave generation, scoring a top-10 hit.

Sgt. Pepper's was an early version of the concept LP, and its popularity (along with that of the Beach Boys' *Pet Sounds*) helped to cement the 'art rock' form within popular music. It made the LP format more essential than the single (brilliantly exploited by the Kinks for *The Kinks Are the Village Green Preservation Society*). The album was also a precursor to, and inspiration for, glam and progressive rock.

McCartney said he came up with the idea of a band that wasn't the Beatles because, 'We were fed up with being the Beatles. We really hated that fucking four little mop-top approach. We were not boys, we were men.'

The album finishes with a puzzle – a track that can be played backwards as well as forwards. Most likely interpretations are (forwards) 'never could be any other way', and (backwards) 'will Paul be back as Superman?'.

is for

SGT. PEPPER'S

Sgt. Pepper's Lonely Hearts Club Band, released in 1967, came at a troubled time for the Beatles, a pivotal point where band relationships were becoming frayed and the relentless schedule of touring was taking its toll. The album was formed from an idea of McCartney's, of wanting to distract from the Beatles' all-pervasive image. George Martin recalled Paul saying to him, 'Why don't we make the album as though the Pepper band really existed, as though Sergeant Pepper was making the record?'. With Martin in charge of production, the album became much more than just a simple record. Experimental, influential, catchy, crammed with great tunes from start to finish, surprising, exhilarating and revolutionary, *Sgt. Pepper's* broke the mould, but without alienating the audience. Quite the opposite, in fact. Some of the Beatles' most memorable tunes work the grooves of the record – elsewhere moments like Harrison's 'Within You Without You' and the extraordinary album-closer 'A Day in the Life' still influence young bands today. Without 'A Day in the Life' there would have been no 'Bohemian Rhapsody' and no 'Paranoid Android'. The cover is iconic, with the Beatles in their famous military-band finery. It features artists and historical figures who resonated with the Beatles. *Sgt. Pepper's* won two Grammys and is reported to have sold more than 32 million copies worldwide, making it one of the best-selling albums in music history. In 2003 it was named the greatest album of all time by *Rolling Stone*.

T
is for

TOMORROW NEVER KNOWS

The last track on *Revolver*, credited to Lennon–McCartney but mostly written by Lennon, 'Tomorrow Never Knows' is arguably one of the most influential tracks of the decade and is, to this day, certainly one of the most mesmerising and challenging songs ever written. A major influence on the sixties psychedelic rock explosion (and the subsequent myriad revivals) and the victim of major sample-pilfering, the importance of the track cannot be underestimated. Two years before the Beatles went to India, the Fab Four were clearly interested in Eastern spirituality, meditation and, yes, drug experimentation (inspired in part by William S Burroughs). The result of their experiments, 'Tomorrow Never Knows', was a transcendant hymn to the higher plane – that groove, the oblique lyrics and all-encompassing spiritual aesthetic. It is one of the linchpin songs for the progression of contemporary experimental pop music, psychedelia and electronica. Consisting mostly of one C chord drone and a C major chord overlay, with a small change at one point to B flat major, 'Tomorrow Never Knows' threw out the idea of conventional pop-music chord structure. Lennon's vocals were fed through a Leslie speaker, normally used to amplify a Hammond organ.

The song title was taken from a comment Ringo made when talking about an incident at the British Embassy in Washington DC, where someone had cut off a lock of his hair. Lennon heard Ringo exclaim 'tomorrow never knows'. The song had a working title of *Mark 1*.

The track appeared in the episode of *Mad Men* entitled 'Lady Lazarus'. It reportedly cost the producers a massive $250,000 to use the track.

Lennon told George Martin that he wanted 'a sound like a hundred chanting Tibetan monks'. The vocals were recorded coming out of a revolving speaker ... prompting Lennon to quip that the same effect could be achieved if they hung him upside down and spun him around the microphone. Lennon later said, 'I should have tried to get my original idea, the monks singing. I realise now that's what I wanted.'

THE TIBETAN BOOK OF THE DEAD

The song's lyrics were inspired by the book *The Psychedelic Experience: A Manual Based on the Tibetan Book of the Dead*, written by Timothy Leary, Richard Alpert and Ralph Metzner, researchers investigating the therapeutic potential of psychedelic drugs.

The drone was reportedly made using a sitar and a tamboura (a long-necked Balkan mandolin). Effects were achieved with reverse cymbals, tape loops and faders, and dials on the mixing desk that panned the music from one side to the other. The Mellotron's flute and string settings were also used.

T is also for

'Taxman'
A song from the 1966 album *Revolver*, 'Taxman' was a bitter tirade against Harold Wilson's high rate of 'progressive' tax in the UK at that time, meaning that the more you made, the more you were taxed (it got as high as 95 per cent if you were in the top income bracket). The Jam 'borrowed' the riff for their song 'Start!'.

...

Thomas the Tank Engine
Ringo narrated the children's TV show *Thomas the Tank Engine and Friends* for the first two seasons, broadcast on ITV in 1984.

...

'Ticket to Ride'
Released in April 1965, 'Ticket to Ride' was the Beatles' seventh number-one single in the UK and their ninth in the US. Written by Lennon, the track was included on the LP *Help!*. It is widely viewed as a turning point for the Beatles, a progression from love songs, covers, yeah yeah yeahs and clichés, to a harder and heavier sound. It was a major influence on power and jangle pop.

...

'Twist and Shout'
Written by Phil Medley and Bert Berns, 'Twist and Shout' was originally recorded by the Top Notes, then taken to the upper reaches of the charts by the Isley Brothers in 1962. It was also covered by the Who and the Tremeloes, but the Beatles really made it their own. It was included on their debut LP, *Please Please Me,* and was recorded in around 15 minutes. Lennon was suffering from a severe cold and the rasping, phlegmy result is one of history's most memorable vocal performances.

U is also for

Unreleased

There are quite a few Beatles' songs that have never been officially released, which pop up here and there in bootleg and demo versions. Among the best of these are 'Child of Nature', the melody of which Lennon later used for his solo hit 'Jealous Guy'; the fabulous stoned groove of McCartney's 'The Palace of the King of the Birds'; 'Circles', a Harrison-composed, hauntingly melodic down-tempo tune; and Lennon's bitter 'The Maharishi Song', a precursor to 'Sexy Sadie'.

...

Ukelele

George Harrison played the ukelele on Beatles' songs and many solo tracks, and often extolled the virtues of the instrument. Tom Petty recalled how Harrison turned up at his house one day and taught him how to play the ukelele. John played ukelele on 'All Together Now', and Paul often played it in his concerts, most notably when he played 'Something' in the Concert for George in 2002.

...

Unplugged

The Beatles Unplugged is one of their most highly regarded bootleg records – a collection of home demos and knockabout jam sessions recorded at Harrison's Esher estate Kinfauns, at a time when the Beatles were said to be falling apart. However, there's little that suggests that on this record (although Starr is absent). What you do get is joyous versions of 'Back in the U.S.S.R' and 'Yer Blues', plus a reggae-styled 'Ob-La-Di, Ob-La-Da', as well as various other curios and oddities.

In October 1963, Ed Sullivan was delayed at London's Heathrow Airport because the Beatles were arriving from Sweden and crowds had started to gather. Sullivan, who had the most popular show in America at the time, made a mental note of the band's name

The Beatles' meeting with Dylan at New York's Delmonico Hotel is lauded as changing the course of musical history, when Dylan introduced the band to marijuana for (apparently) the first time.

The band played two concerts at the legendary Carnegie Hall on 12 February 1964. Keith Badman quotes John Lennon in his book *The Beatles Off the Record*: 'Carnegie Hall was terrible! … It wasn't a rock show; it was just a sort of circus where we were in cages. We were being pawed and talked at and met and touched, backstage and onstage. We were just like animals.'

I ♥ THE BEATLES!

The Beatles' US tours triggered a major influx of British bands, including the Rolling Stones, Eric Burdon and the Animals, Herman's Hermits, the Kinks, Freddy and the Dreamers, and the Dave Clark Five.

Lennon's comment about Jesus has been misreported over the years. He actually said, 'We're more popular than Jesus now; I don't know which will go first – rock 'n' roll or Christianity.' At first there was little reaction, but when the Christian right got hold of it, a series of public burnings of Beatles albums and memorabilia followed. Epstein considered cancelling all Beatles trips to the US because the reaction was so extreme.

U is for THE UNITED STATES

When the Beatles hit America, no one could predict the chaos that would ensue. Music history was being made. Pan Am Flight 101 took the Beatles – accompanied by Brian Epstein, Neil Aspinall, roadie Mal Evans and a few journalists – over the Atlantic on 7 February 1964. The plan was to appear on *The Ed Sullivan Show*, then play a few concerts. They performed five songs on Ed Sullivan and their performance drew an audience of 73 million – an estimated two-fifths of the American population. They would go on to hold the top five positions on the Billboard Hot 100 in April 1964, a record that remains unbroken. The band returned to the US in 1964, '65 and '66, playing to packed-out shows. However, 1966 would see the undoing of the Beatles in America. Someone should have told John Lennon never to take on Jesus in the US, but he did with the comment, 'We're more popular than Jesus now,' sparking an outcry that, although it didn't end their popularity, certainly made enough of an impact for the Beatles to end their days as a live band. Their final performance at Candlestick Park was a success, but didn't fill the stadium. They received death threats and were picketed by the Ku Klux Klan. The incident and ensuing madness would push the Beatles to turn away from conventional rock and roll and to rewrite the rule book, changing the course of contemporary music forever.

V is for VIDEOS

In 1965 the Beatles were feeling the pressure of constantly having to appear on live television. For a heavily in-demand and extremely busy band, the solution was to record taped performances to send to shows. Their early proto-music videos include 'We Can Work it Out', 'Day Tripper' and 'Help!'. The latter was used as the opening for the film of the same name, and also served as a promo for the movie. Shot on a soundstage at Twickenham Film Studios, the clip was sent out to music shows like *Top of the Pops* and *Thank Your Lucky Stars*, which had up to that point been entirely live (or mimed). Clips were also made for 'Ticket to Ride' and 'I Feel Fine', directed by Michael Lindsay-Hogg. All the clips were of live performances. In 1966 the Beatles produced a short promotional film for the song 'Paperback Writer' (in colour!), and three for 'Rain' (the B-side), which were widely aired on new media of the time. 'Paperback Writer', while still a performance video, was performed in the Chiswick House gardens rather than on a soundstage, marking it as one of the pivotal points where a concept clip was created for a song. One of the three clips for 'Rain' took this further – showing the band wandering the grounds with cut-away shots of children playing. The clip was aired on *The Ed Sullivan Show* and *Top of the Pops* in June 1966. The colourful 'Hello Goodbye' started something new, then 'Strawberry Fields Forever' and 'Penny Lane' followed – concept videos in full colour, which featured no singing and no instruments, heralding the future band video. A 'TV Special' was shot for *Sgt. Pepper's*, but ended up being cut down and used as the clip for 'A Day in the Life'.

There was no miming in the 'Strawberry Fields Forever' video because of a ban on miming that had been put in place by the Musicians' Union. The Beatles got in trouble later on when it was obvious they were miming for the 'Hello Goodbye' video.

In their performance videos, the Beatles played around with the visuals from the beginning. Ringo holds an umbrella for 'Help!', and rides an exercise bike for 'I Feel Fine'.

V
is also for

Vietnam War

The Vietnam War lasted from 1955 to 1975 so, by the time the Beatles arrived in the US, it was midway through. The Beatles were opposed to the war and were very vocal about it. The song 'Revolution' directly addressed the situation, supporting the protesters but at the same time admonishing them for the violence of their protests. The stance made the band less popular in America.

...

Klaus Voorman

Astrid Kirchherr introduced the band toartist and musician Klaus Voorman at the Kaiserkeller club in Hamburg, by Astrid Kirchherr. Voorman eventually moved to London and designed the cover art for *Revolver*, for which he won a Grammy. Voorman has had a long career as a session musician. He contributed to many of the Beatles' solo albums and released his own solo album in 2009.

...

Vocals

While Lennon and McCartney had the lion's share of lead vocals, George still managed a significant contribution. Ringo sings on the fewest number of songs, but he was usually allowed an average of one song per album to himself.

Swedish director Peter Goldman made the clips for 'Strawberry Fields Forever' and 'Penny Lane' and recalls how the band would sit in John's Rolls Royce and give advice to (and taunt) him.

The *Magical Mystery Tour* movie is effectively a collection of music videos. Of special note is the clip for 'I Am the Walrus'. The mix of footage, performance, costumes and characters set the template for future music videos.

In the 1995 TV series *The Beatles Anthology*, George Harrison says, in reference to their early music videos, 'So I suppose, in a way, we invented MTV'.

The video for 'Paperback Writer' was played on ITV's *Ready Steady Go!* in June 1966, which was reportedly the first time the show had broadcast footage that had not been filmed in their studio.

W is also for

'Within You Without You'

After he stayed in India with his sitar teacher, Ravi Shankar, Harrison was inspired to write this track, which combined western pop with eastern music, thus helping to kick off the Summer of Love, psychedelia, world music and experimental pop. Critics at the time (and even now) derided it as pretentious and dull. As the opener to the B-side of *Sgt. Pepper's*, it certainly stands out as notably different. However, its legacy continues. It has been covered by Sonic Youth, Patti Smith, Flaming Lips, Oasis and Cheap Trick and, on the Beatles' LP *Love*, it was cleverly mixed with 'Tomorrow Never Knows'.

...

'With a Little Help from My Friends'

Written by Lennon and McCartney, this track was always intended to have a vocal by Ringo Starr. He sang it under the guise of the character 'Billy Shears', and it's hard to imagine anyone else from the band singing the track today. Starr still performs it in concert and, when it was released as a single along with the 1978 reissue of *Sgt. Pepper's*, it charted in the top 100 globally. Joe Cocker covered the track in 1969 and his unique version took the track to number one in the UK.

...

Wonderwall Music

George Harrison's debut solo LP was released on Apple Music in 1968, before the Beatles had split up. It was the soundtrack to the film *Wonderwall*, and featured Indian musicians and guest spots by Ringo Starr and Eric Clapton. The 1995 hit song by Oasis was inspired by the soundtrack.

'Hey Jude' and 'Revolution' (not the versions that appear on this album) were recorded during the album sessions but released as a separate double A-side single.

The BEATLES

Lennon said McCartney's songs for the album were 'cloyingly sweet and bland', while McCartney said Lennon's were 'harsh, unmelodious and deliberately provocative'. Lennon famously said, 'the break-up of the Beatles can be heard on that album'.

Ringo left the band after feeling under-utilised and unloved, and following a spat about his drumming on 'Back in the U.S.S.R.'. In his absence McCartney played drums on 'Dear Prudence'. Starr was eventually wooed back and returned to a studio and drum kit covered in flowers to welcome him back.

On Harrison's insistence, Eric Clapton played solo guitar on 'While My Guitar Gently Weeps'. Clapton gifted Harrison the guitar he used, which Harrison named 'Lucy'.

A bumper 50th-anniversary reissue of the album was released in November 2018. Speaking of the reissue, McCartney told The Canadian Press, 'I haven't listened to it in 50 years. I don't really listen to stuff we did. Then it comes around again (with a reissue). It happened with *Sgt. Pepper*. I go, "Woah, check this out ... those kids are good!" It all comes flooding back.'

is for

THE WHITE ALBUM

The Beatles' ninth UK studio album, released in 1968, had a working title of *A Doll's House*, but ended up being called *The Beatles*. However, the plain white cover with just an embossed title ensured that the album would forever be known as *The White Album*. It was released on the Beatles' own label, Apple Records. The band had written most of the tracks while on their retreat in India, and had taken a much less collaborative approach to writing, allowing their own styles to show through. It followed on from, and kicked against, *Sgt. Pepper's*. The cover was a direct contrast to the highly visual and colourful sleeve of *Sgt. Pepper's*, and the random nature of the song placement was a rejection of the concept LP. The sessions were problematic: Ringo left the band for two weeks during recording; some say that Yoko's constant presence in the studio put a strain on the band; George Martin took a sudden hiatus; and engineer Geoff Emerick vacated the chair. Occasionally though, beautiful things come from chaos and *The Beatles (The White Album)* is now regarded as one of the greatest and most influential records of all time. A double album, it was the Beatles at their most raw ('Helter Skelter'), most experimental ('Revolution 9'), most intriguing ('Happiness Is a Warm Gun'), most jaunty and comical ('Rocky Raccoon') and most wonderfully melodic ('Blackbird'). Controversial, exhilarating, confounding and inspirational, *The Beatles (The White Album)* is a masterpiece and on its release went to number one in the UK, US and Australia.

is for
X-RATED

GOD SAVE THE BEATLES

GOD FOREVER BEATLES NEVER!

BAN THE BEATLES!

JESUS LOVES YOU! DO THE BEATLES?

UNHOLY BEATLES!

Despite their songs frequently being banned by radio stations for drug references and use of words like 'knickers', the Fab Four, compared to bands like the Rolling Stones, mostly appeared to behave themselves – from the outside anyway. However, insiders (especially the Beatles themselves) have plenty to say about their hedonistic times. It seems like, with everything on tap and the world as their oyster, the filthy four took what was on offer and ran with it. Speaking to *GQ* in 2018, Paul McCartney spilled the beans on the early days of the Beatles and their nocturnal activities. McCartney said that one night when they were young, he was in a room with John Lennon and a few friends when one of the friends started to masturbate. Everyone in the room joined in, with various names like Brigitte Bardot being called out for encouragement. Typically, after a little while, Lennon amusingly called out, 'Winston Churchill.' McCartney also talked about sharing a room in the early Hamburg days, which meant that any 'activities' took place in the presence of the other band members. As the youngest, George Harrison was the last to 'become a man'. When he did, in a dark room surrounded by his bandmates, he received a warm round of applause. The Beatles were also known for excessive drug taking. Lennon said, '*Rubber Soul* was the pot album and *Revolver* was the acid.' Ringo later admitted that there were some particularly drug-fuelled sessions. He said, 'When we did take too many substances, the music was shit, absolute shit'.

The original cover of the US album release *Yesterday and Today* featured a rather bizarre photograph, shot by Australian Robert Whitaker, of the Beatles dressed in butcher smocks, holding pieces of raw meat and decapitated plastic dolls. Whitaker wanted to get away from the Beatles' 'squeaky-clean' image and do something more adventurous. The album was quickly withdrawn due to public outrage and the cover redesigned with a more conventional photograph. Known as the 'butcher cover', original copies of the sleeve are now one of the most valuable Beatles collectibles.

Lennon and Harrison (and their wives) had their coffee spiked with LSD by dentist John Riley, later referred to by George Harrison as the 'Dental Experience'.

Lennon and Ono became addicted to heroin in the late 1960s. Ono attributes their ability to kick the habit to the low purity and scarce availability of their supply. John Lennon also used a flotation tank to help. His song 'Cold Turkey' describes the symptoms of coming down.

The famous line from 'I Am the Walrus', 'I am the Eggman', stemmed from a conversation that Lennon had with the Animals' singer, Eric Burdon, which involved one of Burdon's sexual exploits where a girl cracked a raw egg on his chest, which ran down his body, and then she pleasured him.

McCartney recalled to *GQ* a time in the US when a tour promoter asked him if he wanted a hooker. Paul requested two and enjoyed his experience. He also mentioned John Lennon leaving a club to sleep with a married woman, only to discover the husband was watching. But John was fine with that.

is also for

X-rays
While together, the Beatles were banned in Russia and never played there. But nevertheless the Soviets found a way to listen to their music. Bootleg discs were a booming industry, but vinyl was scarce and expensive, so Russian fans came up with the idea of etching tracks onto discarded hospital x-rays. The resulting bootlegs were Beatles music pressed onto flexi discs, along with creepy pictures of broken arms, legs and rib cages.

...

The X-Files
In Season 7, Episode 19 of the paranormal investigation show *The X-Files*, called 'Hollywood A.D', Mulder investigates a murder and finds an ancient pottery relic in a church's catacombs. He tells Scully the legend of the 'Lazarus Bowl', a clay pot said to have etched into its surface the words of Jesus as he raised Lazarus from the dead. While examining the relic using sonic analysis, it is found to contain the lyrics to the Beatles' 'I Am the Walrus'.

...

Xmas records
The Beatles sent spoken messages to their fans on flexi disc each Christmas from 1963 to '69 and all seven were released on a special compilation in 1970. Highlights included 'Rudolph the Red-Nosed Ringo'; a sketch called 'Podgy the Bear and Jasper'; a version of 'Nowhere Man', played on ukulele by Tiny Tim; and an interview between Yoko Ono and John Lennon.

Y is also for

'Yesterday'

'Yesterday' was written by Paul McCartney in 1965 and appeared on the Beatles' album *Help!*. The song originally had the lyric 'scrambled eggs' in place of 'yesterday', a device used by McCartney to remember the melody. 'Yesterday' won the Ivor Novello Award for songwriting in 1965, it was nominated for a best song Grammy in 1966 and inducted into the Grammy Hall of Fame in 1997. In Lennon's 1971 song about McCartney, 'How Do You Sleep', he pointedly says, 'The only thing you done was yesterday'. 'Yesterday' holds the Guinness World Record for being the most covered song in history.

...

Yesterday and Today

The Beatles' 10th album for Capitol Records, *Yesterday and Today* was initially only realeased in the US and Canada and featured tracks taken from EMI UK releases *Rubber Soul* and *Help!*, the double A-side single 'Day Tripper'/'We Can Work it Out' and three tracks from the forthcoming *Revolver* LP: 'And Your Bird Can Sing', 'Doctor Robert' and 'I'm Only Sleeping'.

...

Yoyo

Big fans of Carl Perkins, the Beatles covered his 'Right String, Wrong Yoyo'. The rare recording was an outtake from *Jamming with Heather*, a bootleg of jam sessions from the 'Get Back'/'Let It Be' sessions, when Linda McCartney and her daughter Heather (from a previous relationship, who was later adopted by Paul) were in the studio.

On the cover of the LP, Lennon is seen with his forefinger and little finger raised, a gesture that would later become the standard hand symbol for rock and roll.

'All You Need Is Love' was written by John Lennon and released as a non-album single, but also appeared on the soundtrack to *Yellow Submarine*. In 1967 the song was broadcast to over 400 million people during the first globally televised link-up, 'Our World'. The song went to number one in the US, UK, Australia and many other countries.

Pro wrestler Brian Heffron used the stage name 'the Blue Meanie' and reportedly came from 'Pepperland'.

Some of the characters that appear in *Yellow Submarine* include the Blue Meanies, the Lord Mayor, Countdown Clowns, Apple Bonkers, the Dreadful Flying Glove, Old Fred and Jeremy Hilary Boob.

The Blue Meanies were originally intended to be red, but were changed accidentally by art director Heinz Edelmann's assistant. However, it was agreed at the time by all that blue worked better.

Y is for YELLOW SUBMARINE

As with *Sgt. Pepper's*, the Beatles' 10th album, *Yellow Submarine*, was born from a world conjured up by Paul McCartney. It was the soundtrack to their animated movie made in 1968, directed by George Dunning and based on a story by Lee Minoff (drawing on ideas from Lennon and McCartney). Surprisingly, this tripped-out, colourful, fantastical adventure was born out of despair. At the time the Beatles' relationships were disintegrating and, sadly, manager Brian Epstein had passed away, leaving the band in a managerial and emotional hole. Previous Beatles films had not been so well received, but *Yellow Submarine* was a smash hit. The title song is, of course, also a Beatles classic. Side one is interesting because it was a benchmark for George Harrison's unsung genius. It featured two of his best Beatles compositions, 'Only a Northern Song' (which was left out of the film) and the brilliant 'It's All Too Much'. The album's side two was an orchestral soundtrack arranged by George Martin. However, musically, everything was always going to be overshadowed by 'All You Need Is Love'. The album went top five on the charts in the UK and the US. The original title track on the album *Revolver* (1966), was sung by Ringo Starr and released as a single backed by 'Eleanor Rigby'. It went to number one in the UK for four weeks and won the Ivor Novello Award for the most sales of a single in 1966.

is for

ZEBRA CROSSING

The Beatles' 11th studio album, *Abbey Road*, released in 1969, features one of the most iconic album covers of all time. It was designed by Apple Records' creative director John Kosh and photographed by Iain Macmillan, and is second only to the *Sgt. Pepper's* cover in notoriety. *Abbey Road* features the four Beatles walking across Abbey Road's north-western zebra crossing. The album cover doesn't mention the band's name or the title of the album. The executives at Apple Records saw this as commercial suicide but, as designer Kosh told the BBC in 2009, 'We didn't need to write the band's name on the cover ... they were the most famous band in the world.' Abbey Road Studios, in St John's Wood near Lord's Cricket Ground in London, is still a popular recording studio today, but the Beatles album is its most famous achievement. The album cover art gave the studio a place in history as well as becoming a millstone around its neck. The popularity of the crossing picture endures today. As it is so easily imitated, it brings hordes of fans and day-trippers to snap themselves walking across in a recreation of the iconic sleeve. This causes endless holdups on the busy thoroughfare. On the 40th anniversary of the album, thousands of people packed Abbey Road to be part of a photoshoot on the famous zebra crossing. The crossing was given a National Heritage Grade II building status listing in December 2010.

The famous crossing was dug up for resurfacing in 2018. Hordes of fans gathered to grab pieces of the rubble left behind.

Devoted 'Paul is dead' theorists have found countless references in the cover image: Paul is holding his cigarette in his right hand (Paul is a lefty, so this guy must be an imposter!); joining the dots in the concrete on the back of the album makes a '3', indicating the number of real Beatles; the number plate of the Volkswagen Beetle is LMW 28IF, meaning Paul would be 28 if he were alive (despite the fact that he was actually 27); a black police van symbolises the authorities staying silent about the fatal car accident …

The white Volkswagen Beetle pictured near the zebra crossing, LMW 281F, belonged to a couple who lived across the road from the studio. The car's number plate was repeatedly stolen after the album's release.

Frank Zappa

Frank Zappa was the guy who John Lennon said he always wanted to meet – no surprise really, as both were uncompromising firebrands. Frank Zappa and the Mothers of Invention's album *We're Only in it for the Money* was a clear send up of *Sgt. Pepper's*, complete with a mock *Sgt. Pepper's* cover. Zappa called McCartney to ask permission to make the parody cover, and Paul replied tactfully that it was an issue for the business managers. The cover was delayed for five months, and even then the record label, Verve, moved the photo to the inner sleeve of Zappa's album. Despite this, Lennon and Zappa jammed together onstage at Fillmore East in 1971. Lennon released the recording on his live album *Some Time in New York City*. Zappa said, 'I guess he went in with Phil Spector and mixed the thing with this ridiculous tape delay echo on it'.

…

Zither

George Harrison played a type of zither called a swarmandal on the songs 'Strawberry Fields Forever' and 'Within You Without You'.

…

Zapple Records

Apple Records set up a side imprint, Zapple Records, to release more experimental material, as well as spoken word records. In the end only two albums were produced on this label.

ABBEY ROAD NW8
CITY OF WESTMINSTER

The Abbey Road street sign has been constantly stolen, graffitied and defaced. In a bid to bring down the repeated costs of replacing the sign, the council placed it on a much higher spot of the corner building.

Many people have imitated the cover, including the Peanuts characters, *The Simpsons*, Ren and Stimpy, Kanye West, the Red Hot Chili Peppers and, most famously, Paul McCartney himself, walking his dog on the cover of his album *Paul McCartney Is Live*, the title acting as an excellent pun on the death rumours. Cute fact: the dog on the cover is Arrow, one of the puppies of the sheepdog Martha, who inspired the song 'Martha My Dear'.

Yet more fuel to the fire that 'Paul is dead', in the photo Paul McCartney is wearing no shoes (in some cultures the dead are buried without shoes), and walking out of step with the other members, who seem to represent a funeral procession. The conspiracy theory stated that McCartney had died in a car crash and been replaced with a doppelgänger to keep the Beatles as a viable commercial entity.

Smith Street Books

Published in 2018 by Smith Street Books
Melbourne | Australia
smithstreetbooks.com

ISBN: 9781925418903

CIP data is available from the National Library of Australia.

Publisher: Paul McNally
Project editor: Hannah Koelmeyer
Editor: Ariana Klepac
Design: Michelle Mackintosh
Illustration: Chantel de Sousa, The Illustration Room

Printed & bound in China by C&C Offset Printing Co., Ltd.

Book 86
10 9 8 7 6 5 4 3 2 1